# TO BE YOUNG AGAIN!

poetry today

# TO BE YOUNG AGAIN!

Edited by
Rebecca Mee

First published in Great Britain in 2000 by Poetry
Today, an imprint of
Penhaligon Page Ltd, Remus House, Coltsfoot Drive,
Woodston, Peterborough. PE2 9JX

© Copyright Contributors 2000

All rights reserved. No part of this publication may be
reproduced, stored in a retrieval system, or transmitted
in any form or by any means, without prior permission
from the author(s).

A Catalogue record for this book is available from the
British Library

ISBN 1 86226 584 4

Typesetting and layout, Penhaligon Page Ltd, England.
Printed and bound by Forward Press Ltd, England

# *Foreword*

To Be Young Again is a compilation of poetry, featuring some of our finest poets. This book gives an insight into the essence of modern living and deals with the reality of life today. We think we have created an anthology with a universal appeal.

There are many technical aspects to the writing of poetry and To Be Young Again contains free verse and examples of more structured work from a wealth of talented poets.

Poetry is a coat of many colours. Today's poets write in a limitless array of styles: traditional rhyming poetry is as alive and kicking today as modern free verse. Language ranges from easily accessible to intricate and elusive.

Poems have a lot to offer in our fast-paced 'instant' world. Reading poems gives us an opportunity to sit back and explore ourselves and the world around us.

## Contents

| | | |
|---|---|---|
| On The Seashore | Sylvia Bryan-Foster | 1 |
| Moving On | John Crowe | 2 |
| Thumberlene | Sylvia G Bentley | 3 |
| Reflections On Childhood | Joan Drewell North | 4 |
| Our Glittery Tree | Natasha Piris | 5 |
| Just A Child | E R Croker | 6 |
| A Foggy Dublin Night | E Buckley | 7 |
| Christmas Eve | Christine Isaac | 8 |
| Born Into Purgatory | J Lucas | 9 |
| Mysteries | Karen Lisa Ryley | 10 |
| A Christmas Dream | Elizabeth Leach | 11 |
| Christmas Memories | R Sandford | 12 |
| Memories Of Long Ago | William Barnard | 13 |
| Memories | Sheila Elkins | 14 |
| Reflections Of Childhood | Anne McKimmie | 15 |
| Christmas Remembered | Giovanna Gallo | 16 |
| The Walnut Tree | Monica Redhead | 17 |
| Growing Up | B Symons | 18 |
| Inclusion | Mike Morrison | 19 |
| Africana | Seema Khehar | 20 |
| Memories Of Past Summers | C Champneys Burnham | 21 |
| Garden Verse | Juliet James | 22 |
| Snowflakes in Summer-Time | Jean Mackenzie | 23 |
| Yesterday | L J Harries | 24 |
| Stop Me And Buy One | Fred Bennett | 25 |
| Thoughts Of Long Ago | Maureen Gard | 26 |
| Innocence | Nicola Pym | 27 |
| The Tank Engine's Graveyard | Barrie Allen | 28 |
| Grace | K Maguire | 29 |
| Times Past | D J Day | 30 |
| Great Aunt Sarah's Christmas | Brenda Gill | 31 |
| Fights Through Childhood | Yvonne Sturge Prince | 32 |
| Why? | Sarah Targett | 34 |
| Childhood | Sandra Eros | 36 |
| Please Turn Life's Clock Back! | Paul Ruthven-Lee | 37 |

|  |  |  |
|---|---|---|
| The Coefficient Of Glory | Derek Webster | 38 |
| My Recollections | Betty R Lloyd | 40 |
| My Granny | Derek Relph | 41 |
| Childhood | Margaret Boles | 42 |
| Too Late | Andrew Rochell | 43 |
| Sweet Child | Nadia Nuth | 44 |
| Did I Really Do That? | Gerry Knight | 45 |
| My Old School | J F Grainger | 46 |
| Youthful Haze | Peter John | 47 |
| Northern District | Yvonne Fraser | 48 |
| Reflections Of Childhood | B Jones-Baynam | 49 |
| Hell Down Paradise Row | Kevin D Clapson | 50 |
| My Child | Gordon Harper | 52 |
| Home For Christmas | Kathleen M Hatton | 53 |
| Behind My Chair | Shirley Sammout | 54 |
| Never Forgotten! | Anita Slattery | 55 |
| Contentment | Millicent Colwell | 56 |
| Reflections Of Childhood | Robert Peters | 57 |
| The Road Taken | Michael Apichella | 58 |
| Dreams Of Long Ago | F King | 60 |
| Family Life In Guernsey | Felicity Fonteyn | 61 |
| The Berries | Fiona Higgins | 62 |
| Burning Skies | John Merritt | 63 |
| The Field At The Back Of The House | Megan Guest | 64 |
| School In The 1930's | John Paulley | 65 |
| Nostalgia - Christmas 1943 | Pat Heppel | 66 |
| Reflections Of Childhood | Ivy Russell | 67 |
| My Childhood | Pauline Haggett | 68 |
| Reflections Of Childhood | Catherine Frost | 69 |
| Muses Of The Third Age | Barry Jones | 70 |
| Ordinary Child | J M Harvey | 72 |
| Fishing Trips | R T Owen | 73 |
| Memories Are The Little Things | Yvonne Tyerman | 74 |
| Winter Of 1963 | James Ashworth | 75 |
| Remember Margaret | David Galvin | 76 |
| School Days | G McWilliam | 77 |
| Childhood | Joan Waller | 78 |

|  |  |  |
|---|---|---|
| Childhood Memories | Jan Graver-Wild | 79 |
| Perspective | Reg Akhurst | 80 |
| Once Upon A Time | Donald Futer | 81 |
| When I Was Young | Marion I Goodwin | 82 |
| Reflections On Childhood | J Harrington | 83 |
| Christmas Childhood Memories | Christine Barham | 84 |
| Bramble, Clover And Nettle Grew There - A Childhood | R Wiltshire | 86 |
| Reflection Of Childhood | Rosemary Constance Whatling | 87 |
| Through The Eyes Of A Child | Ian L Fyfe | 88 |
| Funk | Norman Bissett | 89 |
| My World | Daphne Robinson | 90 |
| Father Mine | A Jones | 91 |
| The Days Of Our Lives | Sarah Burns | 92 |
| Rocking Horse | Lorna Todd | 93 |
| Saturdays | Janet Phillips | 94 |
| Playtime | Alison Shepherd | 95 |
| I Rhyme With Bugs | Paul Morris | 96 |
| Christmas | E J Paget | 97 |
| My Aunt's Voice | David Hendtlass | 98 |
| Memories Of Childhood | F Dean | 99 |
| There Was A Time | Betty Foot | 100 |
| Nostalgic Times | Gwyneth E Owen | 102 |
| Memoirs Of Rollicking Ron | R Cousins | 103 |
| Do You Remember - Our Cloud In The Sky | Fay Gale | 104 |
| Holidays Of Long Ago | Joyce G Shinn | 105 |
| Pictures In The Fire | J D M Reeve | 106 |
| The Christmas Shop | Sylvia M Bradford | 107 |
| Dreams Of Childhood Days To Christmas | Charlie Boy Smith F Probett | 108 109 |
| Reflections On Childhood | B J | 110 |
| Down Yonder Valley | Justin Bayless | 112 |
| Christmas Memories | Winifred Warne | 113 |
| Boyhood | John Bishop | 114 |
| Sutton On Sea | Jennie Dawes | 115 |

|  |  |  |
|---|---|---|
| The Children's Christmas Concert | Celia G Thomas | 116 |
| Kids Are Like That . . . | Pauline Pullan | 117 |
| Christmas Memories | Valerie A Cottier | 118 |
| Recollections Of Childhood - A True Story | Elsie Karbacz | 119 |
| My Dog | H Z Billam | 120 |
| Childhood Days | Ivy Skinner | 121 |
| Evacuated To Eire, 1940 | Felicity Gill | 122 |
| Childhood | Jean McVicar | 123 |
| Child Think | Jackie Draysey | 124 |
| The Dawn Of Understanding | Margaret Smith | 125 |
| Ways Wherein Once I Strolled | M Cooper | 126 |
| All Good Things Come To Those Who Wait | Justin Bayless | 128 |
| Looking Back | Mary Baty | 129 |
| Class Politics | Andy Botterill | 130 |
| Innocence | J Walker | 131 |
| Robert T Tyranny | Robert T Collins | 132 |
| Reflections Of Childhood | Em Spencer | 133 |
| The Hermit | Phillipa Benson | 134 |
| 38 Lewisham Park | F Pettit | 135 |

## On The Seashore

One day I went out walking,
And I went along the sand,
Then I found a little Starfish
And I took him in my hand,
I held him very gently
And I'm sure he winked at me,
As if to say 'Please kindly
Put me back into the sea'
So I paddled in the water
And I put him down to swim,
Then he sailed away so gaily,
As I waved goodbye to him.

I found a little Hermit Crab,
His house upon his back,
He was running off all sideways
So I called out 'Do come back'
He turned around and looked at me
With eyes like knitting pins,
He had great big claws like pincers,
Where the Fishes have their fins,
He seemed in such a hurry
That I let him run away,
For I thought perhaps I'd find him
Out again another day.

Oh what a lot of creatures
One can find upon the shore
So I'll come again tomorrow
And I'll try and find some more.

*Sylvia Bryan*

## Moving On

The front garden fence
Orange-brown paint now
Curling
Peeling off
Is the same as when I stood
On very spot
And looked
Some fifty years off
As are
The path tiles
No longer scrubbed
Full once a week
The garden edging
And
The bay window

Only the front door
Has been changed

I am aware of
A memory
Of
A memory

I move on.

*John Crowe*

## *Thumberlene*

I thought I'd buy some lovely toys
For little girls and little boys
Things that I just never had
Bought for me by Mum and Dad
I never had a teddy bear
With loving eyes that stand and stare
I never had a golliwog
To dry my tears, give me a hug
Maybe because there was a war
And people then were very poor
But a posh doll? - - - I had a dream
Dressed in clothes of blue and cream
I wanted her to be just there
With rosy cheeks and flaxen hair
I wanted other girls to say
I'd like a doll like that some day
For I would never treat her rough
Mark her clothes or spoil her muff
A lovely doll so seldom seen
I would have called her *Thumberlene*
But life's gone on, the other day
Somebody special came my way
I bought myself a teddy bear
With loving eyes that stand and stare
And maybe if I hold the dream
One day I'll find my Thumberlene
With eyes that blink and are so blue
They'll say so sweetly *I love you*

*Sylvia B Bentley*

## Reflections On Childhood

Childhood
      - wildhood -
Pristine their world
the heart unfurled
the mind runs free
as the green sea
With no imprinting
of the World's squinting.

      Through buttercup fields
      with a cardboard shield
      to face the Gold Horde
      with a wooden sword
      and a paper hat -
      never doubting that
      Right is Might
      in ev'ry fight . . .
At one with
the brilliant flower
(and the Dark Tower)

      Alone - - -
      yet
      at home
      as never
           ever
                   again.

*Joan Drewell North*

## *Our Glittery Tree*

I think
everyone has gone
mad! We've got a huge,
triangular-shaped tree in
our lounge, just standing bare
in a big brown pot, that's normal if abit big.
But then we watch, with mouths open at the spectacle
when these little light bulbs are being wrapped all around, getting
tangled up, nearly falling off their stool as they near the top-it makes
me giggle!
They jump up
and down when they're in
place and realise they all work
and expect us to do the same! Then the real
fun begins we're allowed to join in, throwing this shiny tinsel,
I think they call it, all over, with strings of gold beads, bows and bells
strung around this big green tree this seems pretty, easy and fun!
Then it becomes abit harder, we're allowed to put on the balls.
Some are shiny, some are glittery
and some are funny-shaped ones!
I put one on only for the others to fall off but
eventually the tree looks like a big wrapped present! And just to
finish it off we throw some thin, long strips of gold and silver and if
that isn't mad enough instead of hiding our presents they put them
all under the tree for all our little eyes to see!
Then to really finish it off they make a big deal about putting what
seems like one of my dolls on the top with wings which they call an
angel but that's what they call me!
And all clap and hooray I don't see what so hooray about that my
favourite part was chucking on the goldly stuff
but my real bestiest bit will be peeping at my presents when everyone
is fast asleep
I think.

*Natasha Piris*

## *Just A Child*

To me you are a garden, in an English lane,
To all you are a flower, refreshing in the rain,
So fragrant are the colours, in your upturned cheek
And pleasing are your gestures, as your love we try to seek
That palest pink upon your skin, confirms just what you are within.
Never ever angry, wherever you may look,
Sincere you are in truthfulness and every storybook.
This flower we see, perhaps in bud
Will bloom to its full fullness, its meaning understood.
The love that is around you, will enhance the joys we know,
Return to us the pleasures, rewards we wish to show.
Live on sweet life, and always be,
A joy to all, especially me.

*E R Croker*

## *A Foggy Dublin Night*

Broken pathways slippery with November leaves,
A child, nib like, dipped into the black inkwell
of a foggy Dublin night.
Trousers patched with flesh,
Frozen feet in sodden runners
racing towards the smell of fresh, cooked food!

Noses pressed to the chipper window,
Hungry mouths breathing a prayer of want
on its frosted pane,
Covetous eyes devouring the fresh, fried fish,
steaming hot, golden brown, crisp and crackling
like the landed leaves in Autumn.
And the chips - long white ships
sailing in a sizzling sea.

Running home again to a hungry world,
Through the ever open tenement door.
The cold bare room,
crowded only with a mother's loving smile,
cold face cupped in the soft warm hands
and a whispered 'Where were ya?'

*E Buckley*

## Christmas Eve

It's Christmas Eve late in the night
The Holy Star shines down bright
Fairy lights through windows shine
Bringing joy this Christmas time
Christmas trees stand tall and proud
As snowflakes fall softly to the ground
Carol singers go from door to door
Casting their shadows upon the floor
Children have laid their sleepy heads
Are now fast asleep in their beds
Christmas stockings hanging full of toys
To give lots of pleasure to girls and boys
Under the trees lie gifts large and small
Bringing pleasure to both young and old
People walk home from midnight mass
Sharing seasonal greetings as they pass
Trudging carefully through the snow
Happy and contented home they go.

*Christine Isaac*

## *Born Into Purgatory*

Unaware, certainly all the pre-puberty years
being classified in some discord,
then, as questioning youngster
influenced by all around,
education and personal interest diverting
gradually aware in the close, home circle
mother's hug so extra soothing
father's ready 'cheerio', goodbye handshake
'cold hands - warm heart'
I've no inkling of any reverse.

Summers 'magnificent,' in the category together
comes summertime's end - variance revealed
surreptitious addition of extra clothes
family and close colleagues unwarranted abuse
'Shape yourself - get a move on!'
Winter's marred with misunderstanding
yet, I suppose, we're each below perfection;
My long, slow, painful awareness
links my mind to the other-worldly,
thoughts and sensation mystify universally.

*J Lucas*

## *Mysteries*

Its coat gleaming like crystal stardust,
The unicorn runs wild and free,
Its spiralled horn is made of silver,
But to see it you have to believe.

Mum always knows what I'm doing,
I don't think she finds out herself.
Does a little bird tell her my secrets,
Or does she know a mischievous elf?

Dandelion clocks float on the breeze,
They're really fairies, you see.
I'll hold them gently and if I'm kind,
They'll grant a wish for me.

I'll wish to be back in my childhood,
Where each sound was the fairies song,
And the wizard that lived in the garden
Sent me sweet dreams the whole night long.

*Karen Lisa Ryley*

## A Christmas Dream

Let me take you on a journey to the land of make-believe
To the world of Father Christmas and every children's dream.
A place full of wonder where dreams really do come true
Where glistening snowflakes softly fall in the snow for me and you
The reindeer run so freely playing games in the snow
Forming patterns with their hooves as they go
Father Christmas and his helpers the elves they work so hard
To bring the gifts requested by children wide and far
They answer every letter sent via the North Pole Star
Containing every dream and wish that every child has sent
They are lovingly collected for a Christmas Heaven Sent
Oh where would dear old Santa be without Rudolph to guide
                                          his sleigh
His red nose shining brightly to light a passage way
If you look closely you will see him in the sky pulling a sleigh
                                          of golden light
Santa yo ho ho ing happily every Christmas Eve night.
He visits all the children tucked up tightly in their beds
Dreams of Father Christmas going around within their heads.
Arising early morning sheer delight upon each face
Father Christmas has visited each and every children's place
No-one can ever take away this magic in which we believe
It lives within us all within our childhood dreams
This wonderful time of wishes and magic that comes true
The world of Father Christmas and the gifts he brings to you
How he gets them down the chimney is a mystery you know
Like the magic of a footprint left in freshly trodden snow.

*Elizabeth Leach*

## Christmas Memories

The blazing log fire glowing
on this very special night
excitement is now growing
filling me with pure delight.
The pine tree so majestic
twinkling lights in fine array
the sights and sounds I now observe
it's almost Christmas day.
Brightly coloured parcels are scattered everywhere
the smell of roasting turkey is scenting all the air,
church bells in the distance each bell it's own sweet chime
carols now ascending at this very special time.
Thoughts of Yuletides long long past
distinctly come to mind
the happiness of Christmas you can quickly leave behind.
As the glowing embers dissolve to shades of grey
the crispness of the morning tells me it's Christmas day.

*R Sandford*

## Memories Of Long Ago

In times of solitude and rest,
The mist of time comes rolling by
With memories of long ago,
Of youthful love and hopes aglow,
Of happy days and joyful times
In far away and sunny climes.

Her name was Ayla, I recall,
She was seven and I was eight.
Her knees were bleeding from a fall;
That's how we met as if by fate.
I cleaned her wounds and felt so tall,
The answer to a maiden's call.
The bravest knight from Camelot
And he was I, Sir Lancelot!

From that day on we were as one,
With halcyon days of sun and fun,
With swimming in the warm blue sea
And eating figs fresh from the tree
And picking grapes along the way,
Ending another lovely day
Beside the blue Aegean Sea.

Nothing changed as years went by;
To each other with hopes sky-high
We pledged ourselves for evermore,
Standing there on that lovely shore.

The time arrived for me to go,
That day was black, an awful blow.
And as the years go flying by
I'll think of her until I die.

*William Barnard*

## *Memories*

Memories when I was young
Keep going through my mind
Those golden days I can't forget
As back the years unwind
Summer days ablaze with sun
And holidays to treasure
Then Christmas came with lots of snow
And gifts brought endless pleasure
And as I sit and think about
My life and what I've gained
It brings a smile back to my face
And the memories that remained.

*Sheila Elkins*

## Reflections Of Childhood

We sat and made our daisy chains down on the
Old bleach green,
We placed them daintily upon our heads
To look just like a queen,
Then played at 'Ring O' Roses',
Then we'd jump across the burn,
We'd grab the 'Sheltie' by its mane,
And each would take a turn,
To see how long upon its back,
She'd let us cling and slither,
Before she'd buck and throw us off,
Oh! happy days the gither!

*Annie McKimmie*

## *Christmas Remembered*

There was a tap on the window one Christmas Eve
What would the children like to receive?
Sweets, they both answered with a gleam in their eyes.
Go to bed now, and you may get a surprise.

They received what they asked for and so much more
When they came down to breakfast and walked through the door.
Their eyes seemed to sparkle at the wonderful sight,
How the room was transformed since they saw it last night.

There was a tree in the corner, with presents below
And a fire in the hearth with blaze all aglow.
There was holly and tinsel and fairy lights
And the toys they were given brought squeals of delight.

I remember that Christmas so long ago
Which children today will never know.
Now, they have toys at any time of the year
But those we had then were both precious and dear.

*Giovanna Gallo*

## *The Walnut Tree*

There was a time, so long ago,
when life was just a haze
then, I remember school
at four, my pen a tool
drawing letters, light stroke
up, and heavy one down,
quite out of fashion now.

We had walnut trees in
our garden, green and fine,
sweet nuts cracked proudly
with our teeth (I still have mine)
Rolled hardboiled yellow eggs
down a slope for Easter's Feast
with innocent bliss.

Another time, another country,
sea, blue clean and cool,
better than any pool,
and I, gloriously free
swam out to sea, watching
small fish, brightly coloured,
no thought of race or apartheid.

I was a happy child, then
carefree days soon ended,
war came, bombs-exploded,
nights spent in air raid shelters
children sent to strange
faraway places.

*Monica Redhead*

## Growing Up

Size two, second-hand shoes -
Feet size one and shoes too loose;
Dull and brown, not shiny black,
Button 'cross the middle, not ankle straps . . .

But daddy put it right! My daddy put it right!
Brushed and spit and polished them, late into the night!
Now my lovely, leather shoes are shiny brown and bright!

. . . Why is daddy angry now,
With fists instead of hands?
Why is mummy crying now?
I don't understand . . .

Daddy brought *a kitten* home -
A black and fluffy kitten home,
Daddy brought a kitten home,
A kitten just for me!
Kept it warm inside his vest,
Snug and warm next to his chest,
For the girl that he loves best -
'specially for me!

. . . I heard an angry noise,
It woke me in the night.
I heard my daddy shout.
It sounded like a fight.
I'll put my pillow on my head
And shut my eyes so tight,
That maybe I won't be so scared
And shiver with the fright . . .

. . . Mummy's face is hurt and bruised.
Her lower lip has swelled.
She doesn't want me 'round, because
She isn't feeling well.
I'm trying to pretend she hurt her face because she fell . . .

*B Symons*

## *Inclusion*

Take care of young girls
who venture by night
so wind swept yet warm
loose wrapped in white

Make time for young boys
who caper and play
their frivolous ways
prepare for work day.

Be fair as they grow
through storm and strife
for many's the fun girl
became the best wife.

Take time with young Ross
when he starts to grow
mature in his ways
he'll show you, you know!

*Mike Morrison*

## *'Africana'*

Conjure up Africa and what do you see?
Misery, death, a lone thorn tree.
But come with me and let us explore
I want to try and open the door

I was born in a land of gold
Where the sun always shone
Where I never felt cold
The magical story must be told.

I grew up in a land so green,
In a place that was a child's dream
The beautiful land - what a scene
I wish that here you could have been.

Lions and elephants and animals galore
The cicadas regular evening encore
Grasslands, mountains, valleys and more
It clearly epitomised a perfect score

A place where children were not a pest,
The more you had the more you were blessed.
Those were the days, simply the best
Living life with a certain zest.

On African soil I was born
Why do I now feel forlorn?
Why did not the childhood stay?
Why are my thoughts altered in this way?

As I look, as I recall
I love Africa, where I learned to stand tall
In pain, in conflict, things may be amiss
But my childhood memories are of sheer bliss.

*Seema Khehar*

## *Memories Of Past Summers*

When I was ten, high Summer meant
Long hours of boring cricket.
It also meant rich luscious fruit -
And I was free to pick it.

I've memories of holidays,
Of sunshine, sea and sands.
With Punch and Judy on the Prom
And military bands.

We'd concert parties on the pier
To which I loved to go.
All that I wore were khaki shorts
As I ran to and fro.

Yet six years later high Summer meant
Long hours, which we'd to stick
At swotting for the exam they called
University Matric.

Then when the days were at their best
In school desks row by row
We looked with fear at papers which
Asked what we did not know.

Come eighty years, high Summer means
A lessening of my aches
And hopefully limp lazy days
Beside Italian lakes.

*C Champneys Burnham*

## Garden Verse

Happy little birds that sing
Welcome the poor traveller in.
Greet the early rising dawn.
Sitting prettily on the lawn.

Once awake you fly around
Skilful flitting up and down.
Coyly tilt your little heads
Tapping at the window ledge.

Flying higher off the ground
Stretch your wings without a sound.
Swiftly soar as skylarks sing
You have truly found your wings.

Gliding over garden gate
Wilful staying out till late
Care not what the days may bring
To be as free as birds . . .
You must find your own wings.

*Juliet James*

## Snowflakes In Summer-Time

Snowflakes tapped on the windowpane
Forming glorious patterns, again and again.
Aged six I stood wide eyed by the door
Shouting 'Mummy, Mummy, it's snowing once more.
Quickly, quickly, come here and see
God sent the snowflakes just for me.
I wanted to see the snow again
And I asked if God would freeze the rain,
Come on Mummy, come and see
Snowflakes in summer-time - just for me.'

*Jean Mackenzie*

## *Yesterday*

Corbies still build in tall trees beneath the hamlet steeple
New black feather bundles edge the nests.
Staccato sounds but they do not wake my loved ones,
Nor disturb their hard worn rest.

Beyond the hill the farmhouse stands,
Focus of a lifelong toil,
In quiet content their span was spent,
Deeply rooted in the soil.

From dawn to dusk of every day,
With kines and plough they worked away,
Untroubled by the world without
Unburdened by the slightest doubt.

Of an evening all gathered round
And sang and sang fine hearty sounds,
Until 'thought for the day' was heard,
Then no-one even slightly stirred.

Memories of those far off days,
Undimmed by War or Peace,
Shine like stars through breaks in cloud,
Revealing joys that never cease.

*L J Harries*

## *Stop Me And Buy One*

Hunched over handlebars
He pedals on as in a dream
'Nice brickettes, snofruits and choc bars,
Large family blocks of ice-cream'.

A crazy refrain, these words run on
Repeatedly through his poor head
As he propels his tricycle on,
Another day's work finished.

Blue and white chequered box
Is now just a frosty-coated void -
Of load of family size blocks,
Choc bars and so on - now devoid.

All sold now after pedalling
Through maze of streets in sun
While boldly inviting
All to 'Stop Me and Buy One'.

He pedals automatically
His mind now clear of trade patter
And so thoughts turn to family
And things that really matter:

That bus ride home down Hackney way
A hot meal that awaits him there
The first hot grub all day -
Cold sandwiches ain't no proper fare.

Those weary eyes straining ahead
The factory now near, pedals on
Thinking of supper and then bed,
Tired Mister Stop Me and Buy One!

*Fred Bennett*

## Thoughts Of Long Ago

So much to remember, so many years gone by
Some of my childhood memories still flash before my eyes.
Whitewashed walls of pebbledash, flaking in the sun
Is what I'd see if I went back to where it all begun.

A small country cottage with cosy little rooms
A staircase, oh so narrow, with lots of wooden beams.
My tiny bedroom window, way up beneath the eaves
To this day it remains there, I see it in my dreams.

The tiny plain backyard
Not a single flower in sight,
Just clean grey concrete
Stark, hard and bright.

Two tin baths beside the door, one large and one small
Each week lifted carefully down from hooks upon the wall.
Kettles of water poured in the tub, to fill it was so hard.
In winter placed in front the fire, in summer we bathed in the yard.

The river flowed beyond the fence, I remember, not that wide.
We had a plank across it to the field on the other side.
Sometimes we played in the water watching tadpoles there
In summer the water vanished and it was dry and bare.

We had bluebell woods to play in, fields in which to roam
Never bored or lonely always close to home.
We had such fun in those days of wide open spaces
The sun always seem to shine on our glowing little faces.

Such memories leave me melancholy, breath escapes in a sigh
Now I look on red brick walls and fences six foot high.
I miss the green countryside, the clean fresh air I lack,
But would it be as I remember, if I were able to go back?

*Maureen Gard*

*Innocence*

Oh, to be young again.
Small innocent feet falling on the adventure,
that is life.
Safe in a cocoon of childhood,
hidden from reality,
protected, loved and cared for,
safe in a world of make believe.

*Nicola Pym*

## The Tank Engines Graveyard

It has just dawned on me of late
that I had been to the tank engine's graveyard.

It was watching those W Audry documentaries
that started me pondering their fate.

Jersey Marine it was, the Swansea Docks end.
All lined-up rusting hulks, ready for the slaughter.
Ready for the white-hot gas powered acetylene torcher.

No faces, no Thomas, Edward or James, but 1471, 2069
3473, 1564, 0987, 7864 on and on in patient lines.

They went so quickly like a locomotive Belsen
without tears or struggling or shouting rages
but odd groups of clambering small boys amazed
that they were allowed to touch those steamy
parts after all those years of merely watching
and underlining numbers in Ian Allan's pages.

Somehow the Bluebell Line seems obscene, a sideshow
that's detached itself from its ancestral dark history
pretending the holocaust never really happened you know.

So rest in peace you soldiers of the GWR we salute
your sacrifice and regret no monument hails besides
your line to mark a grave to etch your names
dear tank engines of South Wales.

*Barrie Allen*

## Grace
*(In memory of her puppy Grace)*

Her parents couldn't fill
The gap nature had left
One lonely child
It was hard to make her
Smile tickle, tickle,
Well it worked for a short while.
Sitting on the stairs
She threw away her doll
Who cares! She cried
One night in despair her
Parents left a wicker
Basket there beside
Her bed. A small puppy
Curled up was dreaming
Of a friend she was lonely
The little girl awoke
So did the puppy to,
Oh its Grace I was dreaming
About you. The puppy licked
her face as they embraced
Into a cuddle and a hug
The pup was puzzled
For it had been dreaming
Of this child too.
No lonely little girl
No more Grace and her
Roll on the floor
Screams of delight yelps
From Grace, parents and
nature had a way to
Replace.

*K Maguire*

## *Times Past*

Our memories of Childhood are with us every day.
Warm Summer sun with bright blue skies, Winter snow and
Frost that nips.
We think of battles and fights we had, and the happy times at play.
The pirate games were wonderful as we attacked the enemy ships!

Seaside trips were always a joy, candyfloss, pier rides and tar!
Dips in the sea and fish and chips - all memories to savour for ever.
The sky at night was wondrous, especially your favourite star!
You pondered these things and stored them all up - and when you
spoke
Of them - people thought you were 'clever'

Trips to the Zoo were wonderful, really exciting treats,
(To see animals so strange and new)
Museums too were awesome with so many treasures untold.
Memories of lollies, liquorice and chews and lovely sticky sweets!
Such a vast myriad of memories to comfort us when we grow old.

*Happy Memories!*

*D J Day*

## Great Aunt Sarah's Christmas

The walk to Ridge Farm was arduous,
Battling against the winds from a surging sea;
Ever fearful the road would flood, before we reached
Great Aunt Sarah's welcoming white washed cottage
The postman greeted us from his rusty Raleigh.
Ruddy cheeked, after cycling for miles with greetings
For farmers, fisher folk and ancient villagers
In the distance, bells pealed from Victorian belfry.
The sound of carolling wafted from manor house garden.
At last the village duck pond came into view,
Plump white ducks and geese waddled towards us expectantly.

Suddenly we saw her, waving a white handkerchief
Her ample figure clothed in Sunday best starched pinafore.
Our weariness forgotten, we rushed towards her open armed,
To be gathered up, kissed, hugged and cuddled.
Once inside the scent of a peat fire and of roasting goose
Filled our nostrils, as platefuls of mince pies
And gallons of piping hot tea were rapidly produced.
A loud knocking reduced us all to expectant silence,
Uncle appeared, Christmas tree held aloft to our resounding cheers.
The excitement mounted, as we were caught up
In creating paper chains; Chinese lanterns
And a huge silver paper star to adorn its branches.

After liberal helpings of goose and Christmas pudding,
Aunt Sarah unwrapped, and lovingly arranged, the crib,
As the familiar words of the Nativity story
Filled us with awe and wonder
From Bible page and warbled carol.
All too soon it was time to journey home,
As flurries of snow fell silently on field and fell.

*Brenda Gill*

## *Flights Through Childhood*

Oh, how I loved the pastures green.
The air so fresh the water I esteemed.
When in my early youth I played
On dear Guyana's soil.
The sandy hills I explored
Picking berries at Wismar.

In the countryside on Essequibo's earth,
I climbed the Guava trees,
Wandered in fields like Adam's Eden,
Sampling fruits galore.
The dark red psydium melted in my mouth.
Such thrilling pleasures they brought.
Mangoes, cashews, melons and more,
From these I took my choice.

Oh, some time ago when I was five,
Mother smacked me on the hide,
Because I was merely presumptuous.
There was a trench beside our house,
Its brown water steadily streaming.
Leaning over gracefully was a tall coconut tree
(Bent perhaps from old age
Or uprooted anchorage).
This challenging tree I climbed.
On finding me out, 'That's the limit,' she said.
So, to the house, I was confined.

Quite soon, my ways I hastened to change,
To regain my freedom days,
To roam with friends and explore
The heritage, my bay.

To you! Guyana, how you shaped me,
With your natural rhythm you taught me.
You Guyana, I have made you
My first romance.
Now when rougher days embrace me
I reflect on your lectures with delight.

*Yvonne Sturge-Prince*

## *Why?*

Why is Daddy shouting Mummy?
Is it because he's drunk?
I want to go to bed now,
But Daddy's on my bunk.

Why does Daddy drink so much?
Is it because he gets mad?
I wish he wouldn't shout Mum,
It frightens me real bad.

'You can go to sleep now Bunnykins,
I've moved Daddy to his bed,
I'll see you in the morning,
Now rest your sleepy head.'

It's morning . . can I come in with you?
My dreams have made me scared,
'Cos in them Dad was punching me,
And now I've wet the bed.

Mummy you have bruises,
And lots of blood on you,
What happened this time, Mummy?
Did Daddy hit you too?

That social working lady's here,
She's waiting at the door,
She won't tell me what she wants
Or what she came here for.

But Mummy, what's a children's home,
Why are you saying that?
Is it like the home that we have
With a doggy and a cat?

Oh no, Mum where's she taking me?
I have to stay with you,
If I leave you on your own,
I worry what Daddy might do!

Please Mummy, don't you cry like that,
I'll go if you want me too,
But remember what ever Daddy does . . .
Bunnykins will always love you.

*Sarah Targett*

## Childhood

At first darkness:
the humming of aircraft overhead,
smell of rubber gas masks.
Walking through dèbris
fear stalked me like
a shadow cast over bombed sites.

'Oh God, our help in ages past'
A frequent rising nausea in school assembly,
perhaps from awe.
A school teacher led me away into the fresh air.

Father and Uncles were photographs in khaki uniform.
There were ration books and sticky gelatine cubes.
My Mother fed the kittens; she wore a floral housecoat.

Then came light:
long hours spent in the sunshine of a wild garden.
We played cowboys and indians clothed in black-out
material and coloured feathers.

Voice of my brother on the landing when he sang with me
in unison from another bedroom.
We stole blossom from the *beautiful* houses,
then ran away hurriedly.

A deserted courtyard was another Kingdom, where one
rode a sledge tugged by a short length of rope.
'Our Princess' chanted two curly blonde boys in confirmation,
as they stroked my waist-length hair.

Rita of the blind German mother took me into her
underground greenhouse and our heads swam
in the perfume of so many blooms.

Childhood was a time of dreamy innocence
pervaded by a faint melancholy.

*Sandra Eros*

## *Please Turn Life's Clock Back!*

I look back and laugh -
All the fun that I had;
Lots of friends and excitement,
I shared, as a lad.

I learnt to be caring
With Deb, my first girl;
I thought of long marriage -
My dreams were a swirl.

I did great at school
And thought of success;
Money - no object,
Big house I'll possess.

'Travel the world,
I'll be rich, see happy faces';
When 2000 comes,
I'll have friends, family, been places . . .

But it's eve of 2000,
Where has my life gone?
Wealth and wife's left;
I've sad face, too, on my own.

*Paul Ruthven- Lee*

## *The Coefficient Of Glory*

At thirteen acne erupted
and insistent gloom fractured school.
The overseer of the physics laboratory
Mr Tyson: specifically impenetrable.

But this autumn Thursday, a memory
which time will never rinse out.

Trapped between tedium and fear, trying
to unriddle the coefficient of expansion
of a metal rod, I glanced outside.
Clouds hurried endlessly across a cold sun.

Then it happened. Unshuttered, sunlight
flared across the school field.

Damp earth and grass were lit as a thousand
spiders' webs rippled for the wind.
Each, hanging with dew,
shone a rainbow light.

The angle was crucial. Sitting awkwardly
I held it, watched it disappear and return.

My Tyson's finger accused
the emptiness of my notebook.
The physics laboratory waited for me
after school; detained for inattention.

Haltingly I shared my vision.
His blank stare was unresponding.

For schooling did not concern joy
and the ineffable,
But the public
and the measurable.

Cycling home in dark, beating rain, I wept.
Poetry had fled. 'A fantasy. Will fade with the acne.'

*But he is wrong.*

*Derek Webster*

## My Recollections

I remember as a child I roamed the fields and Bluebell woods,
Taking in the joys of nature and all her different moods.
Those carefree days when my friend and I to Scotney Castle we would go
And all around the back roads in our innocence wandered to and fro.
There seemed to be no thugs or villains in the street like there are today.
As we went home when hungry mother didn't worry, come what may.
The Hall door was always open with orders for meat and bread
Money in an envelope safe for tradesmen to collect, as read.
And then the second world war was declared on a sunny September day
We wondered what would be in store for us in every way.
Sirens sounded when enemy planes came flying overhead.
If we were on our way to school by friends, indoors we were led.
Shrapnel used to fall from fighting planes high in the sky
So we sheltered where we could, to miss the metal flying by.
One day we saw a German airman bale out of his plane quite low,
He was lucky there were gusts of wind to help him to the field below.
My dad went into the Air Force and was sent to a Scottish Aerodrome.
Mum was a Red Cross worker as she looked after us all at home.
Dad heard of the bombs all around us, so he found us somewhere to stay,
Off went our family on the train - to Grangemouth we found our way.
People were all very friendly, there was great camaraderie about
They seemed to live for the day as their future was in grave doubt.
Although there was a war on, or perhaps because of it,
There is not the friendliness today to compare with that great spirit.
After rationing and shortages of goods the end of the war came at last
We were thankful we all came back to our home after good times, and bad, had passed.

Betty R Lloyd

## My Granny

My granny was a lovely woman
With a hairnet, specs, thin legs
A pin cushion nose and dentures that shoogled
A four foot ten wonder
Who loved me very much

I recall every crevice of her Edinburgh home
The reek of cat mint by the door
The brown linoleum in the hall
The smell of Cussins soap
In the bathroom where I dooked for apples
With a fork on Hallowe'en

I see her budgie, Mickey, pecking millet
Her dead paw's picture on the wall
With a big black hat on
The air raid shelter out the back
With me in it, firing tracer bullets
At imaginary Messerschmitts

My granny was a lovely woman
Who smoked roll ups
Cooked Kraft dinners
And slabs of treacle toffee
That shattered in a hundred pieces

As I did the day that granny died
Her ruined lungs a grim monument
To the cigarettes she loved so much

But now, in a new millennium
I still stare fondly at a faded photograph
Of her, arms folded and smiling, from 1913.

I loved my granny very much and her me
She is in my heart now and always will be.

*Derek Relph*

## *Childhood*

My sister and I
Had a craving one year,
To explore all the haylofts
On the farms that were near.
I remember climbing,
Through holes above mangers,
In ones or in twos,
Oblivious of dangers.
At teatime we'd compare,
The interesting details,
Of the ease or the difficulty
Of our exploration,
We came to no harm,
My daughters have never
Had this fun.

*Margaret Boles*

## *Too Late*

When I was little I wanted to be hugged
I wanted to be spoilt with love and kisses
I wanted to be tucked up in bed so warm and safe
And for people to pass by and give me a wave
I wanted to feel the warmth of my mother's knee
And to play eye spy and see what we can see
I wanted to run in the grass and play bat and ball
I wanted you to be so worried that I might fall
But I was told to stop crying and to dry my face
Not a tear must anyone trace
I got the cane today mum I cried
You must have deserved it she said
I shuddered and wished she was dead
Come on off to school
She would wipe my face with her hankie and say you'll do
It's opening day at school mum are you coming
I'm going to get a prize
I can't anyway I've already been there twice
I brought my prize home and put it under my bed
Not a word was said
I reminded mum I'd won a book but she carried on cooking
And never looked up
I thought one day when I grow up I'll make her proud to call me son
And that's just what I have done
I have had lots of poems published and I am overjoyed
The only trouble is my mother died a long time ago
She died too late for me to show
That I was gifted with words and prose
How you hurt me mum you'll never know.

*Andrew Rochell*

## Sweet Child

I didn't want to do it
(Be an Angel in The Play)
But Teacher says I've got to . . .
And Nativity's today!

So they've backed me into silly wings
An' a skimpy little dress -
But how they'll drag me on the stage
Is anybody's guess!

I've just outgrown my 'terrible two's'
(But still can scream and shout)
And a tantrum from this three-year-old
Would bawl the choir out.

And *if* they get me up there,
I'll just slump there, and look glum -
The sulkiest of 'angels' -
Who just *sits*! And sucks her thumb.

No glossy family album
Will reflect *my* shining hour -
Just tears glistening on my cheeks,
When I frown . . . and stamp . . . and glower . . .

With parents arriving already,
I've just spotted Mum and Dad!
But, if *they're* hoping to cajole me,
I'll just pout and cry, 'Too bad!' . . .

. . . Unless those sweets my Dad's got
Could maybe be for me . . .?
If I brighten up . . . take centre stage, . . .?
An' outshine the Christmas tree . . .?

*Nadia Nuth*

## *Did I Really Do That?*
*(Excerpts from my youth; 1960-1969)*

I would like to tell the story of days plucked from my youth,
Tales of woe and glory - but tales that are the truth.

The first that comes to mind, now, was first time I skipped off school,
Frightened by the bullies, with threats to push me in the pool.
Headmaster came to see me, and found I was not sick,
And when he heard my story, the bullies got some stick.

And then there was the green paint from Mr James' gate;
He went in for his dinner, and we did not hesitate.
We slapped some on the fencepost; we slapped some on the gate,
I've got a good idea, I'll slap some on my mate.

So green he was from head to toe, like the Thing from Outer-Space.
It's my turn now - it looks like fun - I'll slap some on his face.
Well, you can sure imagine what mums said to their sons,
Out came the turps and scrubbing brush, which gave us red sore
                                                          bums!

And then there was the coloured man; such a lovely chap,
He's a new guest in our country - but we did not know that.
He chased us down the street for climbing on his bike;
We thought he'd try to eat us, or roast us on a spike.

But he did not want to hurt us, or see us shed our blood;
I suppose that when he chased us, it really did some good. *Or did it!*

*Gerry Knight*

## *My Old School*

I shall always remember when I was taught at that council school
With its box like desks and those wooden champlike stools
Upon a large peg hung a cane with a shepherd's hook
The teacher was reading and scanning our names in a book.

We always stood together in that crowded assembly hall
And the school regulations behind a frame upon its wall
There was a large playground that would ring with screams
Its we had our football games I never played in the team.

The boys did woodwork, the girls made those small jam tarts.
We always played in separate yards we were always kept apart
The girls played with a skipping rope, we kick an old tennis ball
The only time we were together when we sang in the hall.

I stayed at that council school thro' my childhood years
The headmaster's favourite pastime was tugging at our ears
And for my daily punishment I was given six of best
I was the Glass room fool the dunce who never passed a test.

That was a happy day when I left that local council school
Written upon my leaving card this boy will always be a fool
To this day I can see that cane with a carved shepherd's hook
And that stern old teacher had entered my name in his note book.

*J F Grainger*

## *Youthful Haze*
*(Devoted to 'Tereza Balakova' Lover of the Poetic Mind)*

When I was young
I wanted to be
Like 'Grouch Marx'
A joke to see.

When I was young
I wanted to be
With 'Genral Custer' and
                His Seventh Cavalry.

When I was young
I wanted to be
A 'Super Hero'
        Fighting tyranny.

When I was young
I loved those days
Filled with adventure
My mind in
        Poetic haze!

*Peter John*

## Northern District

I attend school in Perth at the Northern District,
Where the teachers tend to be strict
Our old school to me is number one,
Where they try to teach education as fun.
In primary one we learn the basics. A, B, C,
And counting numbers 1, 2, 3.
In primary two we explore colours: reds, green and blue,
We learn how to make things, paper and sticky glue.
Taught are we to practice to read from interesting books,
Bright pictures of jungle animals. Have a peek! Look.
In primary three we have learnt tables and to write,
Letters for English adding more numbers to get it just right.
Moving up to primary four,
Hi-tec, history, computers, projects galore.
Another year over and into primary five,
Busy our learned class with homework we thrive,
At last senior pupils in primary six and seven,
To prepare us for first year. Sad to leave,
Happy days of our primary school haven.

*Yvonne Fraser*

## *Reflections Of Childhood*

'I love you', words I often heard,
As I lay in my bed,
The love so false, just like him,
These words I always dread.

So many years have passed since then,
I thought often, I'm no use,
The only thing I was good for,
Was work and sex abuse.

It took much help and real love,
From those who really cared,
Of times of facing life that's past,
And times that I did dread.

The years have helped to heal the wounds
Have helped to bury shame,
I've learned that I am not the one,
Who should carry any blame.

So childhood memories for me,
Are best put behind, forgot,
What's more important, is what's ahead,
To the life that I've now got.

*B M Jones-Baynam*

## Hell Down Paradise Row

We were dragged there by our parents, all us tots of age
The dread of 'School' comparable, with entering Hell's rage,
Why were we forced to go, had we done some heinous crime?
That awful trial of 'School, day one', has passed the test of time.

When kids noticed tears well, in every grown up's eye,
For miles they surely heard the screams, as Mums kissed us goodbye.
A Banshee called our 'teacher' appeared and bellowed 'quiet!'
She did not look like any Mum , and so, began the riot.

Infants bolted here and there, in vain bids to escape
Then the Master just like 'Dracula,' arrived in his black cape.
He ordered us to 'line-up, but not in single-file,'
We quaked to hear 'we put beginners, in a crocodile.'

Imagining the day had come, we all would meet our doom
We trembled all the way to 'class' and peered inside our tomb.
Blackboards on walls had 'mystic signs' the likes not seen before
Brown wooden forms and tables, stood on our dungeons floor.

'Sit down, class,' said the 'Banshee', but no one would succumb
No 'Yes Miss' to her 'Death list', each name called out stood dumb.
We held our 'code of silence' until a break for play?
But barbed-wire round our jailyard, foiled mass breakaway.

We did not take the 'poison' school cunningly disguised
It looked like milk, but we knew, it was really 'cyanide',
The same applied to dinner, though most of us felt famished.
'Suspicions proved', when back in class, sick tots who ate, had
                                                    vanished.

When the last bell sounded, to end our days despair
All had either wet themselves or messed new underwear
With the trauma over, I hugged Mum tight and swore
'Never to be bad, Oh Mum! don't bring me back no more.'

On the journey homeward, I burst out loud in tears
When Mum declared 'You're going back at least for ten more years.'
Will time erase those moments, we came through Hell together,
Or, is the shock of 'School, dayone', set in chalk forever?

*Kevin D Clapson*

## *My Child*

My child locked away
By more than bars or doors;
By shame.
Rejected and neglected,
Without nurture or friend.
Nightmare's substance,
I was afraid of you,
My prodigal child.

Emaciated and condemned
By another's guilt;
Sharing only your grief with me,
You have waited,
Waited for my 'Welcome Home.'
So the dream,
Fearful awakenings,
Our only shock filled contact.

Now my child
*I embrace you,*
And we are embraced
By Another's love.
Accepting,
Respecting,
Nurturing me,
Both man and boy.

*Gordon Harper*

## *Home For Christmas*

At home for Christmas always was the hope.
We'd decorate the house on Christmas Eve.
Holly behind the pictures; in the hall
Hung Chinese lanterns, older, I believe
Than we, the children; Father called the best
'Old Glory', elegant in gold and red,
And six or seven others, nightlight lit
When dusk set in, seemed magic overhead.

No relatives lived near or came to stay,
Nor had we telephoned our friends to greet,
But cards and presents brought them very near,
As Christmas carols sounded in the street.

As we grew up, a pleasant custom rose,
A glass, part filled with potent home-made wine
We lifted, as my father checked his watch
As did our relatives, for stroke of nine;

Then 'Relatives and friends!' he gave the toast
And so we drank, knowing that Christmas Day
For those few moments, gathered us as one,
United, though so very far away.

May dear ones lost, perhaps within the year,
Gone 'home for Christmas,' freed from grief and pain,
Unseen, but felt, in warmth of constant love,
Be 'Home for Christmas' in our hearts again.

*Kathleen M Hatton*

## Behind My Chair
*(Dedicated to Dominic Chad)*

There's a man behind my chair, whoever put him there?
Was it tender loving care, with angels flying everywhere?
There's a man behind my chair, is it all so very rare
That he should visit me behind my small settee?
There's a man behind my chair, I pretend that I don't care,
Can't bring myself to stare, nerves tell me I don't dare!
There's a man behind my chair. Is he good or is he bad,
Or is he there to oversee *all* there is of me?
There's a man behind my chair, he gets right into my hair;
Yet life I couldn't hear without him standing there.
There's a man behind my chair, a monkey on my back,
Or perhaps one o'er the eight, a sudden nerve attack!
Did I cause the visit when he thought he'd come and stay?
Am I being haunted or simply is my mind at play!
Until I extradite this force, I'll pretend that I don't care;
Yet I'd suffer such remorse if he left me unaware.
An empty space within my room would fill my very soul with gloom.
I owe a lot to thoughtfulness within this wild affair.
I invite him 'Stay forever', the man behind my chair,
'With you I'm never lonely, with you I have a friend;
'til someone says 'I love you' - with you I'll just pretend'

*Shirley Sammout*

## Never Forgotten

As an only child,
My world fell apart when seven,
Being told my best friend -
Had been taken to *'Heaven'*.

I did not know what to do,
Everything to me seemed lost,
No doubt at that age,
You would feel the same too,
A nurse she wanted to be, and help mankind!

Natural thoughts *'Why'*,
Was *'God'* so unkind?
She is forever in my heart,
With memories and love,
Such a lovely childhood dove!

*'He'* took her to a place of peace and ease,
Never to fear or be in pain again,
That is what I learnt to understand,
And have joy to know she has no more pain,
And eternally with the *'Lord* does remain!

Many a time when she comes to thought,
I feel tears in my eyes,
And a little sad - but for childhood friendship
Am forever so glad!

Though not as a profession -
*'God'* guided me to take part,
Years ago in what she could not,
And through it contentment have got!

*Anita M Slattery*

## Contentment

When I was young I used to skip, jump and run
I raced around on my bicycle till the setting of the sun
We played around in fields and woods and paddled in the stream
Then lay on grass and talked to each other of our future dreams
Sometimes my eldest sister would wake us up at dawn
To go mushrooming, near the farm where they grew the corn.
We had to cross the river which then was very low
We held on to the little ones who were oh! So slow!
We wore our old black daps to protect us from the stones
And other smelly things that had been pushed or thrown.
Before we went to play each day we had jobs to do
Mostly running errands or cleaning shoes for school
Shelling peas or pickling beans or getting rid of weeds
But as soon as we had finished out of doors we'd run
To run up to the fields and have a bit of fun
Or go picking bluebells or violets in the wood
Anything, anywhere, we stayed as long as we could
Soon though we would get hungry, chase each other home
Our eldest brother made sure we did not far to roam
And dad's were very strict then and called us in at dusk
We were made to wash ourselves, and say our prayers, a must.
On Sundays we were quiet, painted or read our library books.
Helped to get the dinner, then to Sunday school (with sour looks)
Because we had to wear our best and best behaviour too.
We'd hurry home to Sunday tea, drat! Visitors, one or two.
We didn't have birthday parties, because we were too many
But because we had each other, we didn't need to envy
In Autumn we picked blackberries for Mama to make some 'jam'.
On fireworks night we had garden potatoes and Dada's home cured
                                                                                   ham.
We eat them round the garden fire and sang till the stars came out
We were very happy with life,
       And you'll wonder why?
              No doubt.

*Millicent Colwell*

## *Reflections Of Childhood*

Mid November, first fall of snow;
Deep, crisp, glistening brightly.
Snow tyres on cars,
A solitary Moose.

'Excuse me, would you like your driveway cleared?'
A couple of dollars earned here, a dollar there.
Move on to the next house,
Distribute the evening's earnings.

School playground now becomes an ice rink,
Children skating instead of playing.
Toboggans now being worked overtime,
Children's laughter heard against a dark sky.

Leaving the snow-covered airport
To arrive at Heathrow in the fog.
No snow here, where's the snow?
Different country, different planet?

Strangers here, strangers there, who are they?
Some are related, some are not.
A cuddle from one person, an introduction from another,
Where am I? Who are they?

The journey 'home', cartoon scenery passing by,
We turn a corner, are we 'home' yet?
On arrival 'home', greeted by more strangers,
Finding solitude in an upright piano.

Two years on having now settled in,
First fall of snow generates mass excitement.
Children scampering into the playground.
What's wrong? Haven't they seen snow before?

*Robert Peters*

## The Road Taken
*(For Maria)*

Our teacher stood before us. His faded black cassock hung from thin shoulder blades like worn out drapes. Wispy ashen cables cross-hatched his creased forehead; dense blue cordage bristled on the back of his mottled hand as he clutched a stub of chalk. 'Ahem.'
Like grazing cattle staring at a passing car, the class looked up.

Only the day before, I found his photograph in a yearbook. A head-and-shoulder profile, all the rage during the Jazz Age. He had been named head boy for the Year 1928. His hair was glossy in those days; a pomaded, peaked, pompadour. His eyes were lucid; curious, direct - not shielded beneath sore red lids and a thatched brow. The Great Depression, the War, and generations of lusty school boys lay ahead.

David Hamilton dug his elbow into John Barns. 'Sir, what made you become a - a teacher?' He wanted to say priest, but David said teacher. My friends rolled their eyes at the question. But I watched the teacher as a blackbird watches a gardener turning friable black soil with a spade.

The teacher glanced at each boy's face until he saw mine. I thought the light in his eyes smouldered, like the cherry red coals of a fire banked early on a winter's day and then forgotten. I looked at my hands. 'Well, Sir?' prompted Hamilton. 'Open your books to page 51, please,' was all the teacher said. The boys groaned. Gradually, the chatter and page-turning ceased. Silence descended as we read 'The Road Not Taken' a poem by Robert Frost. The only sound was the tic-ticking of the clock below the crucifix. My eyes skimmed the clean line of words until I reached the last stanza:

> *Two roads diverged in a wood - and I - I took the one less travelled by,*
> *And that has made all the difference.*

I thought of the young man in that picture in the yearbook. He might have chosen any road - why the road of a priest? When the bell had gone, I remained behind. 'Sir?' My teacher arched his eyebrows. 'What was the other road - I mean the road you didn't choose?' He smiled. 'Oh, there never was another road. It only seemed to be there.'
'Thank you, Sir' I said stiffly. I picked up my book and left the room.

'Christ Almighty, where've you been?' It was David Hamilton. I started toward him. Then I stopped and walked the other way. 'Oi! Where're you going?'
Without looking back, I called over my shoulder, 'Somewhere different.'

*Michael Apichella*

## Dreams Of Long Ago

When I was just a little lad
I lived with my folks, by a big main road
I'll always remember that quaint old house
As my very first abode.

The trams used to rattle by
And make the windows shake,
Especially in the dead of night
They would keep me wide awake.

We shared an outside loo
Which really was a bore,
Newspaper hanging on a nail
No bolt inside the door.

When the snow lay crisp and deep
I would have such a lot of fun,
Building a giant snowman
Whose eyes and nose, were a stale currant bun.

I would put a hat upon his head
A scarf around the neck,
Dad's old pipe in its mouth
It looked real grand, by heck.

I used to go to the reccy
Now named Mandela Park,
To watch the trains go by
With all their fire and spark.

But now I've grown much older
Times seem to go, from good to bad,
How I wish for the days, of long ago
When I was a little lad.

    *F King*

## *Family Life In Guernsey*

The Isle of Guernsey was our home
And we were wont to play
Around the garden, on the lawn
And in the fields of hay.

A quiet meadow by the stream
Where daisies strewed the grass,
With clover and bright buttercups,
There sunny hours we'd pass.

No tractors would disturb the peace,
For horses pulled the ploughs.
The winding country lanes were green
Beneath the leafy boughs.

In summer time we went to swim
Down on the sandy bays.
Beside the deep blue silken sea
We gladly spent our days.

This tranquil time was soon to end.
Bombs and artillery,
As they advanced towards our shores,
Split up the family.

I do not wish to dwell upon
Those days of war and strife,
For some were killed and others spared
To seek a better life.

Those years of grief are in the past.
They cannot harm us still
Nor spoil the ever present now
Unless this is our will.

For in the present Love is here
Releasing us from fear.

*Felicity Fonteyn*

## The Berries

Aye, whit a time we had at the berries
Workin' the land for fun and for pennies
We made no' much money but fun there wis plenty
Hard work as weel for me and for Jenny

Och the sun it aye shone richt braw on us then
We never would mind whit it wis tae see rain
Wi' oor pieces an' cheese and a bottle o' pop
We started oot early and ne'er did we stop

But whit did we dare wi' all o' oor money
It went tae oor mithers an' that wisnae funny
Fir new shin an' claes for school it did buy
An' pencils an' rubbers were a' pit by

Aye Jenny an' me we had fun in the sun
For lazin' aroon I wisnae the one
But if we were lucky - an we were noo an' then -
We'd catch sicht o' the lads as we went doon the lane

We'd laugh and we'd joke a' the way doon the road
An' never oor folks would they ever be told
O' the fun that we had wi' the lads long sine
Aye it wis braw and aye it wis fine

An' noo that I'm older by a few years or more
The thocht o' the berries mak's me want more
But tho' the spirit is willin' the body is no'
So I'll jist remember hoo it wis long ago.

*Fiona Higgins*

## Burning Skies

*A blistering rain of terror,*
*the hated enemy sends this night.*
*We lie in corrugated iron shelters*
*with friends we might not ever see again.*

Our tainted souls cannot forget
those lean and languid days of burning skies;
when we breathed the dust of fallen brick
with smarting eyes from spewing fumes.
And how those dark plumes of towering death
tasted in the acrid breath of night.

Now I ease my mind from ever waking sights
of winged black messengers of hate,
like specimen beetles upon a velvet sky.
Pinned by cruciforms of searching lights
and gobbed upon by dancing tracers of fiery phlegm,
coughed from the raging throats of angry guns
upon a distant hill.

Now, I brush away these residues of war
and swallow the tranquillising pill of silent peace
for long, delicious nights of worthy sleep.

But still, can I ever keep those times before
as touching nursery rhymes to tell the young,
of how we lived and loved beneath a violated land,
or should I hold my tongue?

No . . . they'll understand.

*John Merritt*

## The Field At The Back Of The House

An oddly shaped, uneven plot,
Deep puddles forming after rain,
Rough and marshy, our delight,
Squelching under wellingtons.

With long-stemmed yellow buttercups;
Cowslips peeped out shyly at its edge;
Beneath its trees and bushes,
Gleamed silken celandine.
Abundant daisies for our chains,
Streaked magenta for our games,
As prettily we decked our hair,
Princesses for the day we were.

A wilderness field, our magic place,
Where no one came to cut the grass,
Two horses shared our paradise
And munched long hours to keep it neat.
They placidly watched us at our games,
Swishing out at summer flies,
Sharply alert when mother called
To feed them kitchen waste and bread.

And we oblivious, played our games,
Regardless of what time would steal.
The sun hung there in cloudless blue,
For us, to light and warm our days.

*Megan Guest*

## *School In The 1930's*

We walked to School through rain and shine,
No thoughts or cares of cars or swine;
In wooden desks we took our seat,
The stove in room gave us some heat.

We learnt our tables off by heart,
It was the way our day did start;
When questions asked we raised our hands,
If misbehaved, in corner stand.

The nurse she came to check our hair,
If someone spoke they got a stare;
We used our boards with stick of chalk,
All classes quiet, there was no talk.

The inkwells filled at start of week,
There was no place for classroom sneak;
Our weekly tests all marked in class,
If day was good we played on grass.

At lunchtime stand to say our grace,
Then eat our lunch and wipe our face;
We learn, recite and draw our maps,
We race off home and wear our caps.

At home we change and run to farm,
We do our chores and stay from harm;
When family tea is served and clear,
'Tis homework time or face some fear.

Our Teachers great, they loved us all,
Respect for them, made us grow tall;
With decades gone since schooldays past,
They gave me food, for life to last.

*John Paulley*

## *Nostalgia - Christmas 1943*

In the chill darkness, I finger the telltale bumps,
An orange, some crinkly walnuts make the lumps
In a worn woolly sock, ribboned in red,
Tied to the brass knob at the end of my bed.
Much too early to light my stub of candle.
Gingerly, I creep to the door, turn the handle.
A gnawing cold fills the stone-floored house,
I shiver and scurry like a mouse
Back to the snugness of my mattress of feathers,
A welcome cocoon in the wintry weather.
For days the postman has trudged through the snow
Bringing cards and letters from friends we know
Back in the city, where bombs forced us to flee,
My mother, brother and I now evacuees
With an elderly aunt in her cottage of thatch.
Now a stirring, steps on the stairs, a lifted latch,
At last Christmas Day has begun!
Now for some breakfast, a few presents, some fun!
At the wooden table, cups set out for hot tea,
Small piles of presents for m y brother and me.
A Girls' Crystal book, a diary, a fountain pen.
My brother has a Rupert Annual, a fire-engine with men!
Iron pots on the black-lead stove begin to spit,
One holds the Christmas pudding with threepenny bits!
There's a plump farm chicken with sage and onion stuffing,
Everything on ration, yet we lack nothing.
Fresh grown vegetables, a boiled carrot cake,
Paper chain decorations, Mother helped us make.
After tea, the wireless - Christmas Day's been fine,
A game of cards, then cocoa, into bed by nine!

*Pat Heppel*

## *Reflections Of Childhood*

When Christmas passed, my sisters faced
a gloomy month ahead,
but I was born in January
so I could smile instead.

        For many days I'd think and plan
        how best to spend my day,
        when school was done and I was free
        to hurry home and play.

Mother would always let me choose
what we would have for tea,
and often I would ask for shrimps -
a favourite dish with me!

        How special were our birthdays then -
        how different today,
        when we look back on one more year
        So swiftly passed away.

*Ivy Russell*

## My Childhood

Reflection of my childhood is not happy ones?
For I was an adopted child
Given to people too old to understand
They had wanted a daughter so bad, to go with their son.

When I wanted to play outside the garden gate
I was always told, *No* and had to watch others at play
Longing to be with them, getting dirty yet and also having fun
Not staying in that smocked dress, and laughed at by others
For children can be so unkind at times!

When I got older things still stayed the same
You can't go out with that girl, she's not the same as you
She comes from a rough family
And of course that will never do.

At school I was only good at art
But told, this is only for fools
It will not earn you money
So now go and learn something new.

Cooking was what I also like to do
But buying things to take to school
That I could learn how to bake
Dad never liked it because mother had not made it
So in the bin it went, Oh what a waste.

So my reflections are not happy ones
Now I wish I were a child again, now they have more fun
Gone is the old ink well upon the old wooden desk
Now it's computer and going onto the Net!

*Pauline Haggett*

## *Reflections Of Childhood*

We were poor when we were children
Like so many at that time
But we loved our parents dearly
They were so caring and so kind
We had our happy days
With spinning tops and beads
With hoola hoops and marbles
These things filled our needs
There were times when we were hungry
The cupboard almost bare
But we knew that though so little
We always had to share
Times were hard - we knew not why
But because we loved each other
We always 'just' got by.

So in pensive mood
It's fair to say
These are some of my memories
Of childhood days.

*Catherine Frost*

## Muses Of The Third Age

The older I get, it seems
The importance of the present diminishes and the past increases,
That my third age (according to modern dictates if not to
                                                   Shakespeare)
Is becoming closer to my first,
Not that the second age was not momentous -
College Days, Falling in Love, Marriage, Children, Career -
Thirty-four years compacted into a mere eight words,
But now a bridge is building itself in retrospect;
Childhood friends, forgotten, overlooked,
Now impinge with increasing regularity on my mind,
The remembrance of a parental embrace, long cold these fifty years,
Returns now unbidden, warm and affectionate,
Woodworking tools, inherited from a father
(Accountant by profession, carpenter by inclination,)
Used now, summon up his spirit, ever watchful, ever interested in my
                                          carving and shaping,
Some fleeting fragrance from a long closed musty cupboard,
Catapults me back to childhood,
Where a duster-turbanned, apron-embalmed Grandmother,
Cob-web deep in long overlooked corners, dusts, polishes,
                                        springcleans,
Or,
Let me smell the bitter-sweet smell of paper and print in a book-sale
                                                   book,
And once more I am that little boy of four turning the pages on an
                                               uncle's knee
The nose is a wonderful organ of nostalgia.

What, I wonder, might all this mean?
An advance into a second childhood?
The first gentle stirrings of approaching senility?
As the final years beckon does the cycle of life turn its full three-sixty
                                                  degrees,
Do we return from whence we came?
In the natural order of things are we born and do we die as children?

I ask because I do not know the answers,
I ask because I am curious -
Another indigenous trait of childhood I suddenly realise!

*Barry Jones*

*Ordinary Child*

Always Mona, she was always best
in his eyes, daughter of the year
and I, a poor-run second, hanger-on
by dint of blood - the tolerated one.

Why aren't you more like Mona? And I felt
a rush of envy, biting back, I shrugged,
nonplussed, I couldn't answer, couldn't tell
exactly what it was I should have said.

So silence judged me distant and aloof;
love froze like hopeless fish in winter ponds;
I dreamt I was a changeling with a gift
for camouflage - this ordinary child

who someday would delight him with her kiss.
He didn't seem to think it cruel to scorn
my efforts - crush ambition with a word,
looked awkward when I played at being close.

Yet one day, when I was sick as I recall,
he sat beside me, wordless, while he drew
a peacock with my crayons - green and blue -
the colours shone, the moment magic still.

I never was the apple of his eye
but age has claimed him, mellowed year by year -
on duty visits we're all nods and smiles,
and make believe this warmth was always there.

*J M Harvey*

## Fishing Trips
*(Dedication to my father)*

I went fishing with my father when a child
These times were carefree Days to me
But to my father, these days were nothing but toil
Digging for bait lug and king rag was his best
He used a rowing boat in rough weather or mild
He has good Cod, Holes or Marks you see
Two in line on the right and two on the left not to fail
He could go to the same place at any time, he passed the test
He would fish all day up to dark even the wind was wild
A sack full of fish of all kinds will be
Ready for customers Bob or two they were not spoil
After a day of toil, my father's welcome rest
There were countless days when I was a child
Of fishing trips For my father and I
A friend of mine would come along to enjoy
A time of messing on the straits more or less
One time my friend and I, while looking after the boat while idle
We stopped rowing talking and when we looked to see
We found ourselves upon a massive rock, what ills
And after much heaving and pulling, the boat with my guest
We were afloat again, father did not know of our plight
*Oh!* I miss those wonderful days when I was a child
I learned a lot by Father ways of how things should be
And how he rowed that boat against the tide it was just a toy
He was honest and truthful and he was truly blessed.

R T Owen *(A Beaumaris lad)*

## *Memories Are The Little Things*

Around the world in eighty days
Elastics, kirby, Tigg.
Rush my tea and out again
Feeling bloated like a pig
But when your young
You do these things
Without any care
Forget your coat, no need
For gloves
Are me mates still there
A country ride on my bike
With my buddy Steph
We'd feed the ducks
And have a picnic
Till there's nothing left
Going out for day trips
With sister, mum and dad
beaches, zoo and castles too
were the bestest times I had
And in the car we'd sing along
and play eye spy with them
Brown girl in the ring
Was best by Boney-M
Swimming on a Sunday
for a lark around
Texan bars and Cabana's
Oooh! They were just sound
I look back, what seems long ago
And nice thoughts come to mind
And hope our daughter Tegan
Has memoirs of this kind.

*Yvonne Tyerman*

## Winter of 1963

1. Gliding down the hillside
2. Over the frozen snowflakes
3. My sledge gathering speed
4. Home to a hot mug of soup
5. In front of a warm fire and crackerjack.

*James Ashworth*

## *Remember Margaret*

Remember Margaret way back when, we were young and fancy free.
Of summer days upon the green and the old horse chestnut tree.
The hours we spent in the timbered barn and the orchards leafy
green.
We had no cares what the future held nor worries of life unseen.
Remember Margaret the river where we would often swim and play,
Just children having innocent fun throughout the summer day.
Then when the winter time began we saw the river's frozen flow.
And we would wake upon the morn to a countryside of snow.
Remember Margaret Christmas time with excited anticipation in the
air.
Aunt Bertha's yule log's and mince pies and mistletoe that was always
there.
Close your eyes and let your memory stray to Aunt Bertha's small
front room.
Imagine the smell of Uncle Stanley's pipe with its heady smoke
perfume.
Remember Margaret the spider gate, down at Seaton Place.
The house that bridged the river Stour and the cascading old mill
race.
The buildings where the home guard drilled the cartoon pictures on
the wall.
Of Hitler Goring, Mussolini too before the allies caused their fall.
Remember Margaret time moves on and of the pictures there's no
trace.
The Horsechestnut tree has fallen down and our world's a different
place.
But remember Margaret time stands still in the recesses of your mind.
We can still recapture our childhood days and hold them motionless
in time.

*David Galvin*

## *School Days*

The happy days that I recall
From primary school to junior
My final days as a senior 'swat'
Were just a little sadder
Because I loved the life I led
Many good friends not bad
I respected all my teachers too,
For the good times I did have.

My favourite days were school days,
From one term to another,
Especially during summer time
When teams played against each other.

The sporting trophies were on display
In the hall where we all stood,
Singing our favourite hymns.
That made us feel good.

Studying maths and history,
And other lessons too.
We would benefit when we grew up
This was the goal we had in view.

*G McWilliam*

## *Childhood*

Daddy is a sailor goes out to sea
Mum works all day and can't be with me.
When I come home from school I am alone
So I go to bed and pull the cover over my head
Soon mum will come home and light the gas mantle
Fish and chips out of newspaper tastes so good.
In Sunday School we are told God loves us all.
When out playing I lost my ball.
Dad and mum love me so much and I
know that God loves me too.
I am getting big. I am six soon
And wonder what my present will be.
A pair of new shoes or a coat and hat
Mum will choose what is best for me.
I cannot see God but I know he is there
keeping me safe as I sit on the stairs in the dark.
I hope it is bread and dripping for tea.

*Joan Waller*

## *Childhood Memories*

My childhood memories are Mother, Father and Baby Bear,
A loving happy childhood without a single care.
Girls have curls and lots of Dollies,
Cradles and prams and I even had a Collie,
Who was a stuffed dog who was very jolly,
Boys had trains and some had brains,
They liked horses too, but only a few,
We played Weddings, Mothers and Fathers, clowns with red noses,
Ring a ring of roses and statues and poses,
School days happy, exams and teachers snappy!!
I was always polite, but had to be quiet,
Because Daddy liked to snooze, after a booze,
Said Gran with a sigh and a tear in her eye,
Her memories of childhood that were so very very good.

*Jan Graver-Wild*

## *Perspective*

Above my small head
your words float from you
inside a cloud of this and that
grey happening of the day
and with your shifting feet
into that distance
of strange and far-off people

so in my small head
what those things mean
I cannot think or say

left to myself
big letters of the alphabet
could tell me of the slow blink
of the elephant's eye
close dots on dominoes
or the rainbow suddenness
of snowflakes on a red rose

but when you come back
in my small head I understand
that suddenness and closeness
hand in hand.

*Reg Akhurst*

## *Once Upon A Time*

Once upon a time it was, many years ago,
Someone wrote a story, you should really know.
It's all about a little child, born down on a farm,
In a cottage near the meadows, there amid the country charm.

As the seasons passed each year, the child enjoyed them all,
Snowflakes in the winter, then a snowman built so tall.
Then the sun of early spring, shedding brightness on the day,
The little buds upon the bush, signs of summer on the way.

The flowers in the meadows, and the harvest of the corn,
Filled the child with happiness, so glad to have been born.
Playing in the hayfields, paddling in the stream,
With all the other play-mates, in a land of dreams.

Amongst the sheep and cattle, the horses on the ploughs,
Climbing up into the trees, swinging on the boughs.
Sitting by the river, an old jar on a string,
Catching little minnows, in the jar when they swam in.

Playing rounders with your friends, hopscotch on the lane,
Mother calling you to tea, now it's time to end the game.
For along the lane came father time, passing on his way,
Childhood days for you have passed, I heard him gently say.

I answered to the call of time, I always did my best,
Like my parents as before, was again with family blessed.
Looking back upon those days, they really were so fine,
Now so many years ago, it was once upon a time.

*Donald Futer*

## When I Was Young

When I was young I would walk for miles
through farm gates and over stiles.
I would walk down quiet lanes, and across fields so wide
With no-one but Mother-Nature at my side.
I would sit by a stream, with water so clear,
and if I kept really still, little fish would swim near.
In the spring I would pick wild violets and primroses on the way
and take them home for Mother's Day.
I could walk by hedgerows and past many farms.
I could walk alone and come to no harm.
I have lived in my home town all my life,
and in that time have become a Mum and wife.
The country lane is now a dual-carriage way
The fields have gone, factories have come to stay.
Where the farm's once stood alone and proud,
are housing estates with children shouting loud.
I'm sad that others will never see,
The places that were so dear to me.
But I will tell them about my special times instead
As no developers can take away the memories that are
                                                in my head.

*Marion I Goodwin*

## Reflections On Childhood

At 5 years old I loved going to school
They said I seemed quite bright
I was very quiet and well behaved
And never got into a fight
I loved to read 'Tales of Sam Pig'
And play netball as centre half
I know the ball reached the other team
That's because I was short, don't laugh.
I was never chosen for the school choir
Well my voice was very small
I remember the school photo being taken
And standing high, I thought I would fall
At arithmetic I was a whiz
I remember six feet made a yard
I neafer hadd truble whith speellen
And at Xmas, no-one sent me a card.
Well I thought my sewing was good
Like dog's teeth the teacher did say
Then we were all taught to knit
Middle row confusion my needles turned the other way.

*J Harrington*

## *Christmas Childhood Memories*

This Christmas poem penned by me
And written just for you
Tells how in my childhood Christmas past
You made all my fairy dreams come true

I remember how at Christmas time
We'd hang in all the rooms
Shining lametta and paper chains
And in the corners coloured balloons.

We'd decorate the Christmas tree
With lights and toys and glittery balls
Flaking it first with cotton wool
Resembling a world of woodland snowfalls.

On top of our green and fragrant tree
My little doll fairy we would sit
Dressed in her white net curtain gown
You'd specially cut and made to fit.

In the lounge both you and I
Would place a table of Christmas drinks,
Port and sherry and ginger wine
And games like Lotto and Tiddlywinks.

On Christmas Eve I'd go to bed
Full of excitement in one so young,
Waiting for gifts, I knew would be there,
Filling the sack on the bed I'd hung.

Early in the dark, cold morning hours
I'd wake to find my pillowcase
Bursting full of crunchy parcels
Filling every vacant space.

Darling Mother, you made my Christmas
All that a child could ever hope it to be,
And now that I'm older, I'd like to think
I'm the special daughter, your love made me be.

*Christine Barham*

## *Bramble, Clover And Nettle Grew There - A Childhood*
*(Dedicated to Memory of Sally Larner)*

In the days of horse-drawn bread van and rag-and-bone men
There was an acre of wasteland near the pub called the 'Chestnuts'
Where we played our games and puffed acorn pipes in our den
And won our 'battle' scars, grazes, bruises and cuts.
For it was there that we became cowboys and indians, soldiers,
                                         vikings and knights
Amid dumped furniture, mattresses, newspaper and wooden beer-
                                         crates.
Played marbles and jack-stones, flew handmade kites.
Made skimmers from dumped lino and catapulted at tin-cans and
                                         plates.
Played football, cricket, tig-ball and rounders in season,
Pedalled our bicycles and raced 'Dinky' sports cars down bare
                                         slopes of a pit,
Witnessed the annual burning of Guy Fawkes for treason,
Collected empty pop-bottles to take to *Outdoor* for wagon-wheel three
                                         pennybit.
Flew model balsa aeroplanes and slung green cane darts - skyward
                                         aiming,
Tried to catch butterflies and frogs.
Practised balancing on car park tubular railing,
Saw the odd looking chap nick-named woolly with his collection of
                                         stray dogs.
Rusting prams supplied the wheels for trolleys - our 'chariots of fire',
Car seats for bouncing on before fun-castles they do now inflate.
Obsolete wirelesses and gramophones we smashed for magnets and
                                         copper wire
-The wasteland our learning ground - after the clang of school gate.

    R Wiltshire

## Reflections Of Childhood

Everyone knew *Sunday* began the week,
well rest day really, best clothes, chapel, visitors to seek.
*Monday* Brought hustle and bustle with school which I loathed, rules
and time keeping were a terrible load.
*Tuesday* The fishmonger came by on a bike
we lived far from the sea, it was quite a sight.
*Wednesday* I loved joy of joys, 'School Friend' came, cream buns for
tea, mum had bought them just for me.
Six o'clock found us clasping coins, as cries of its coming made a
noise, the mobile chip van moved into view, ringing its bell, but we
already knew, the smell wafted down from the top of the hill.
*Thursday* Was grown up night with mum, the chapel sewing meeting
had begun, news and gossip did abound as did the clacking needles
sound.
*Friday* Near the end of lessons, just my music teachers visit, I wished
I'd practised all my scales, now I'd have to bite my nails.
*Saturday* With chores and play at rest, Dad brother and me listened
to the wireless.

*Rosemary Constance Whatling*

## Through The Eyes Of A Child

I look back on my tender years, when I was young - so long ago.
The years have rolled on by so fast, much quicker than you know.
I try to imagine what it's like, to be an innocent - meek and mild.
I'll write these words as though I see, through the eyes of a child.

My name is Stefanie Michelson and I live in a big old house.
At night it can be spooky, when it's quiet like a mouse.
In Winter when it's windy, and it rustles leaves and swirls,
It really can be scary for all us little girls.

It rattles windows and the doors, as I try to say my prayers.
Was that a noise I heard just now, coming from the stairs?
I huddle beneath the blankets, as the footsteps come my way,
It's only mummy! -she's brought my drink, and for a while she'll
                                                            stay!

Sometimes I lie awake in bed, and listen to the rain.
Drumming on the cars outside, and off the windowpane.
The old tree in the garden is creaking in the night,
Its eerie branches form shadows, in my room so dim of light.

Imaginary claws reach out as though to touch my face.
My little heart is pounding and my pulse begins to race.
Eventually I fall asleep, until another dawn.
The wind's subdued, the trees are still, the night-time shadows gone.

I love the snow in Wintertime, and the fun that it will bring,
Playing with my little friends, but soon it will be Spring.
I long for Summertime to come with the sunshine in the sky,
To watch the waves at Whitley Bay, and the seagulls flying high.

*Ian L Fyfe*

## *Funk*

The boy stood on the burning deck,
Afraid to jump and break his neck,
Afraid that, since he couldn't swim,
The hungry sea would swallow him.

Afraid of sharks with dorsal fins,
Large appetites and bloodstained grins,
Afraid to go aloft, below -
That dizzy height! That golden glow! -

Afraid to launch the rowing boat,
So ended, molten creosote.
No, not heroically dying,
But much more stoically, frying.

(No need of psychoanalysis
To diagnose the lad's paralysis.)

*Norman Bissett*

## My World

In the silent night at the stars I gaze.
As I lie in bed - my thoughts lean back
to memories of bygone days.
In a country town, little I knew
of the sorrow and strife all around
in a war torn world.

Perfect at night was the peace I had,
lying between sheets, crisp and clean.
Trusting (as children do)
in my 'invincible' Mum and Dad.
All was well in my little world.

The mind wanders - I feel dismay
For countries where starvation now
is the order of the day.
Victims of cruelty and ignorance.
They too, are part of my world.

The love of many waxes cold.
Lord, where is your Hand in all the chaos?
Yet Satan knows his time is short,
I will see, as through darkened glass
until I reach the next world.

Prince of Peace, I lie, wrapped in your love
The perfect love that casts out fear.
No pain or darkness Lord, can part us
and I shall sleep, as when very young,
untroubled, in a troubled world.

*Daphne Robinson*

## *Father Mine*

From greatness to dependability
This then the continuing voyage of discovery
A man who is so much a contraction.
Humorously savage, radiantly warm
A man to love dearly a man to despise
His resentment matched by his generosity.
How could one so young fathom the complexities
He is so proud of my achievements, (seemingly)
But all too familiar to the growing threat that I pose
How would he cope with my continued thirst for knowledge.

His stare unflinchingly steel, no longer warm
Grip as strong though less friendly.
Deep seated opinions torn
By uncertainty in an ever changing world
Come on Father mine let memories unfurl
I remember bicycle rides, the waltzers twirl
Your strong hands extend like tentacles of calm
Placed on sun scorched shoulders
On endlessly hot summer days,
Your teaching me life's bending ways
Don't give up on me now, reach way back, way beyond
Imploring your thoughts to respond
Then surely I shall see what is vital to me
A reminder of what was you *Father Of Mine.*

*A Jones*

## *The Days Of Our Lives*

We splashed in the river on a load of old tyres
and ate sandwiches out of a tin,
we drank weak squash from saved plastic bottles
and argued about trivial things.

Our ribs poked out from under our shirts
We had brown arms and legs from the sun,
We sang our own songs as we sat on the bridge,
We had to make all our own fun.

We caught minnows in jam jars down in the stream
and sometimes caught tadpoles with nets
we took off our shoes and ran in the fields,
and jumped on the farmers haystacks.

We painted the junk that we found in the pit
and cycled for miles with no effort at all,
we swam in the river with the swans and the trout,
we mixed with the rich and the poor.

They filled in our pit and cut down our trees
and put No Bathing signs in our pond,
but what does it matter, we are all grown up now,
those days of our lives are all gone.

*Sarah Burns*

## *Rocking Horse*

My mother is a rocking horse
Sits in a corner
Rocking
Hair's straggled in a pony-tail
Painted face cracked
With a glazed expression
Rocking
Like wood
Rocking
Rocking horse mother
Split-lipped, coffee growing skin
Rocking back and forth
Dazed for days

Used to be alive
Till a baby came
Baby in a basket
Daddy in a rage

Now my mother is a rocking horse
Sitting rocking
Mind a maze
Can't hear me calling
Can't see me crawling
Falling, falling
From my rocking horse mother's
Cracked paint gaze

These are my rocking horse days.

*Lorna Todd*

## *Saturdays*
*(As I remember)*

Down on the farm
Every Saturday morning
I would go to collect the eggs
Getting the chickens out of their beds,
Then I would have to clean them out.
The droppings I would pile high
To dry them out in the clear blue sky
It's good manure, or so I was told.
It will make good crops grow.
Then, I would have to feed the pigs
Snorting and snouting all around.
And for doing this, I would get half a crown,
When I went home, my mother would say
'Off with your clothes, I've not got all day.'
The tin bath would be in front of the fire
To scrub me clean, from the smell of the farm,
My hair would be washed, my back would be
Scrubbed, and my face would be shiny and clean.
After I dressed a meal would be ready,
Of fresh laid eggs, and home-made bread.

I'd put my money safe in a jar
For one day I was going to be rich,
Even though I was only six.

'People worked really hard for their living,
but they were always loving and giving.'

*Janet Phillips*

## *Playtime*

A face at the window
Glaring outside,
Hands on his hips,
Legs astride.

The street becomes empty,
He looks on with pride,
A child cowers behind him,
She's lonely *inside!*

He's sent them away!
He's done it again!
The sound of silence,
Increasing her pain.

It's time to fetch Bobby,
Janet and Pam,
So she does have friends?
*No!* an imaginary *Sham.*

A face at the window,
Dreams of the day
When someone will call,
Can Alison play?

*Alison Shepherd*

## I Rhyme With Bugs

At school, it was never mentioned,
Smoking was the worst thing you could do,
Many people got suspended,
For having a quick drag in the loo.
What could I be?
Sixteen, time to look for a job,
You've got to do things right,
And that means earn a few bob.
Alcohol is now the enemy,
Drinking cans in bus shelters
And causing trouble.
This lasts a couple of years
Till you break the bubble.
What could I be?
Pubs and clubs are now the scene,
Mixing with people who are lean and mean.
Some of my friends are now
Or have been jailed,
But it's not entirely their fault
They've failed.
It's everywhere
All different kinds
Enough to blow
the toughest of minds.
The future looks very bleak for some,
It wasn't their intention
Or their idea of fun.
What am I.

*Paul Morris*

## *Christmas*

In the days of long ago
Esme and Jim played in the snow.
Wrapped in warm clothes
Very excited
Christmas is coming
We are all delighted
Mummy put candles
On the tree
Lighted up and all aglow
Do not touch
Because there hot you know
At night Jim and I put toast
On the long toasting fork
In front of the fire
Sat in the dark all aglow
And very excited
For Father Christmas
Is coming you know
A glass of wine
A mince pie too
And a pile of pennies to
Pay Father Christmas
From my carol singing money
You know.

*E J Paget*

## My Aunt's Voice

A train rattles off
its full vocabulary
moving on its noise along a line of nettles
below blocks of flats.

In one of these
a disused sound
waits our sudden bell,
an intimate richness,
my aunt's voice.

Hauled by larynx
onto Austrian tracks
it engages
and uses again its heavy articulations,
crosses points of mum's memories
and reverberates
in tunnels of my infancy.

Her voice presses
dust-swirls in a stroke of light
but leaves no print . . .
and no forensic art
can find it out,
not even by fond thought.

*David Hendtlass*

## Memories Of Childhood

Sun in the summer,
Snow in the winter,
Bluebells in springtime,
Autumn's gold shimmer,

Leapfrog and hopscotch,
Maypoles and skipping,
Netball and rounders,
Tops to send spinning.

Bonfires and fireworks,
Skating and sledging,
Warm smell of baking,
Crumpets and cocoa,

Dark Christmas mornings,
Bright golden pennies.
Games round the fireside,
Books to enrapture.

Memories of childhood
Viewed from a distance.
For those simple pleasures
Thanks be to God.

*F Dean*

## There Was A Time

It was time to leave
It was time to go
A time of presents, friends and snow
It was a time to cast away
Now was a time for me to work and not play.
We had shared moments of teaching
Which reflected the world's beauty
And they were far reaching.
Taught the magic of music and the
beauty of art.
Was taught that all things had a start.
Taught that bridges first had to
be planned
When bridges were made that had to
be manned.
Manned by people with true purpose
in life
And through all things there would
be strife.
Gently and deeply my school touched
my heart
And I dreaded the day when I would
depart.
The day came at Christmas time and I
was held in a dance
I was held tightly and how we did prance.
He looked into my eyes and saw the tears
of despair
His hand held mine tightly to show
his care
He also was sorry that I had to go
My love for him has lasted that it was
so long ago.

He was a brilliant head teacher that
really cared
His learning and his expertise he
carefully shared
He was a great teacher and he led
me right
And through his manner I was led to
the light.
We gripped hands tightly and all his
love was in this
And at the age of eleven it was as a
passionate kiss.
In him I saw the depth of a caring man
And in him the workings of God's plan.
We sang Auld Lang Syne, the day
was now past
But the memory of its passing will
always last
It was love that had taught my heart
to sing
And it was love that gave me everything.

*Betty Foot*

## Nostalgic Times

Christmas is a time to reflect
On Christmases of long ago
Sledging down Bryn Hyfryd field in the snow
Laughing merrily with our cheeks aglow.
Father putting up the garlands and the mistletoe
Never knew until later years what it stood for
Until someone kissed me on entering through the door!
Going carol-singing around the houses
My brother in his knee-length trousers
Wearing his hob-nailed boots
Which gave off sparks when he scraped them underfoot.
Feeling with our feet the presents at the foot of the bed
Gifts of books, diaries and fountain pens
Mother had filled our stockings with an orange,
Home-made treacle toffee and small toys
My what a noise!
Waking up in the middle of the night
With such excitement-eating everything in sight.
My youngest sister with her dolls pram and I with a pot doll
Walking together to meet friends, Glenda and Phyllis.
Both donned in their fair-isle hats and mittens.
Yes, such happy memories to remember
And to forever treasure.

*Gwyneth E Owen*

## Memoirs Of Rollicking Ron

Oh happy times, innocent childhood fun
Bedtime stories - being tucked in by mum
Making kites, learn to make them fly
Sweep them off the ground - into the sky

Fishing - a penny cane for a rod
Hedgerow searching for a caddy strod
Bow and arrow with tightened string
Fire . . . but never hit a thing

Play marbles as we walked to school
Fag cards knocksie down, against a wall
We used boxes or cans as our cricket wicket
Runny nose wiped on sleeve - others would pick it

For conkers we climbed Horse Chestnut trees
Childhood was spent with scabs on our knees
Played five stones, Hopscotch and Tin Can Cop
Grubbed around for bottles to spend threepence in the shop

Holes in our jumpers, shoes and our shirt
Hands and legs covered in wonderful dirt
These childhood memories - stored away forever
Ask if I'd change them - the answer is 'Never'

For the kids of today it does seem a shame
All they have is a video and the computer game.

*R Cousins*

## Do You Remember - Our Cloud In The Sky

'Twas was Easter morning
When you held my hand tight,
We had a long walk
The world seemed
So right.

Do you remember
The cross shaped
Cloud in the sky
We imagined it was real
As we stared, at the sky.

Back then I knew your closeness
Could never be broken,
'Blood is thicker',
Some say.

I miss you now
Not a day passes by
When I don't remember
Our clouds in the sky.

*Fay Gale*

## *Holidays Of Long Ago*

How well I remember those days of long ago,
when off to the country for four weeks we would go.
The sun seemed to shine the live long day,
there were so many fields and places to play.
Wydnam, Summerhouse Hill and Bradford Hollow,
trees to climb and trails to follow.

Our room at Gran's had a window to the sky,
where you could lie abed and watch clouds scurry by.
We would check each day for rain or sun,
looking back, it was all such fun.
We'd be of to Weymouth for a day by the sea,
paddling all day and then home for tea.

Sunburned backs, white with camomile,
'You wouldn't listen!' said Mum with a smile.
It happened each and every year,
we would burn ourselves and shed a tear.
Those holidays with my brothers so long ago,
are memories sweet and they warm me so.

*Joyce G Shinn*

## Pictures In The Fire

Daddy's working in London,
Many miles away;
Mother and I sit by the fire,
It's twilight, the end of the day.

'See, it's the magician's castle
On that dark crag over there,
The fire from a dragon guards it;
Approach it if you dare!'

'A princess is kept in the tower,
But look, dear, can you see where
A knight on his steed is arriving -
Magician and dragon beware!'

'He raises his sword, slays the dragon;
Magician, you're next, is his cry;
They fight; now the knight has triumphed,
The magician is left to die.'

'He rescues the princess, they're happy,
She rides on his horse with pride,
Now, dear, it's your turn, what do you see?
Does the princess become his bride?'

'I see a big, dark cavern -
On the walls jewels shine in the gloom;
The floor is covered with treasure -
Can we take some and bring Daddy home?'

'Listen, that's the sound of our bell,
Saying someone's at the door.
Look who it is! Daddy's come home!
We won't let him go any more.'

*J D M Reeve*

## *The Christmas Shop*

I was a child again - in pigtails and bows,
Fat dimpled cheeks, shiny red nose,
Sparkling soft eyes, wide-open with glee,
Stopping and gazing, wanting to see.

I was a child again - expectant, naive,
Wondering, happy, glad to receive -
Every bright colour, each sight and sound,
Knowing that surely, treasure was found.

I was a child again - enthralled and entranced,
Gazing at dolls, dressed and enhanced.
Lights were a-twinkling, jingle bells rang,
Teddy bears slept, angel choirs sang.

I was a child again - believer in dreams,
Impossible aims, fantastic schemes,
Choosing with care, presents and toys,
That Santa would bring to good girls and boys.

I was a child again - transported . . . sublime -
Into a world without money or time,
Where joy is the motive, love is the key,
And people will live in true harmony.

I was a child again - remembering when
Jesus was born in a crude, draughty den,
A child who would lead, instruct and obey
Was God's greatest gift on the first Christmas Day.

*Sylvia M Bradford*

## *Dreams Of Childhood Days*

I set here alone in my ow easy chair, and think uv the things wot I did,
Wen I walked t'skewl, in sunshine an rain, jiss a hornery snottie nosed kid,
We din't hev no trafik t'wurry us then, no cars orl over the rood,
So we cood bowl hewps, and spin tops an the like, yiss livin wooz ever so good,
We din't lock ower doors, wen we went inter town, an we din't hev no feer uv no thug,
Well, cept ow farmer Giles, if we went in his fild, corse he'd cut us aside uv the lug,
The reezun we din't lock ower doors up at nite; that worn't fer the trust wot we feel,
No, if sumwun cum in, hew shoon'ta bin there; there's nothing there fer him tew steel,
Yiss livin wooz eezy in yeers long ago, wen I lived longer Muther an Dad,
We din't hev much uv money an such, But much happiness we olus had.

*Charlie Boy Smith*

## To Christmas
*(A Child's Lament)*

Tell me, where does Christmas go?
Does it vanish like the snow
When all the world becomes my friend
Tell me, why does Christmas end?
When they said that Santa came
Tell me how he knew my name;
Tell me how that this can be,
How did he come to know of me?
Will that bright and shining star
That came travelling from afar
Come again for me next year?
Mother says: 'It will, my dear
If you keep your hope and trust
And your faith - of course, it must!
Then, once again there will be
Christmas chiming merrily!'

*Frank Probett*

## *Reflections On Childhood*

I was a baby born just after the war.
Making the family up to fine
It was very difficult, I am sure,
For my parents to survive,

I reflect on being so unsettled
Lonely and so blue.
I sensed my parents problems - struggles too,
Yet they tried to hide them not to show what was true.

Many strange people looked after by some.
Different environments. Oh? how I missed my mum,
She was out working
To get money to live.
There was never any shirking
They had so much care to give,

And then there was Christmas
Which they made so special
Which really made up for the rest,
At making this event magical
They really were the best,

There wasn't much money- sparce presents.
Only a little tree.
And dad would be Santa - mostly for me
Pillows were left, all full of love
I used to believe they came from above.

Dad put lights all over the house
Every one enjoyed them, even the mouse
It was a Christmas Grotto - I do recall.
Happiness felt by one and all.

I really don't have to reflect too far back
Dad gave us our fantasy until God took Mum
                                        to his shack,
This was not too long ago
How well I can recall,
My parents helped me realise
We are only grown up children after all.

*BJ*

## *Down Yonder Valley*

I look out where down yonder valley
Where a boy ran in the pure winter air
Made tracks to and from school to late lunch
As was provided and then late to class
Where he learnt his lessons and ran for his school
He ran up the hills; the log stairs and the 'ski slope'
Along 'the Elms' across the bridle path with care
As you also in the country air would pant for breath
                          and breathe out smoke
As on some occasion you would race properly and go
Back, and have tea and iced buns at some other school
As from your visit would appeal and race won
Later in the year you would look for the same
But be told 'We had tea and a stale bun when we
                          came to you.'
And indeed they seemed to have found the very ones
Although they seek no prizes here
They merely went down the supermarket and there they
                          were
He took some small piece of change from his own
                          pocket
Is that all it's worth
I mean to run cross country for your school he seemed to
                          be saying
As we ate our humble scones and thought not to gloat
                          too long on whatever win.
We might have lost or won.

*Justin Bayless*

## *Christmas Memories*

Christmas was a special time
Shop windows all aglow
Coming down on Christmas morn
To a lovely Christmas tree
We didn't get too many gifts
As we were rather poor
But we enjoyed the things we had
And didn't look for more
Dinner was quite special too
The best in all the year
With a great big roaring fire
And lots of Christmas cheer
We played snowballs in the snow
Made our feet and fingers glow
Everywhere was snowy white
Such a clean and pretty sight
These are my childhood memories
Of many years ago
Although much older now
My memories set me all aglow.

*Winifred Warne*

*Boyhood*

Racing days, chasing days,.
With eyes as wide as the morn.
When knees and emotions
Were constantly grazed and
Trousers and loyalties torn.

Giggling days, bruising days.
Days ruled by pennies not pounds.
When cycles were horses
And bean sticks were swords and
Reason was still out of bounds.

Searching days, probing days,
Days when carpets were decks,
When treetops were mast heads
And questions were waves and
Only the answers were wrecks.

Naive days, boastful days,
Innocence mingled with pride.
With teardrops and laughter
A blink from the brink and
Dignity nowhere to hide.

Airy days, weightless days,
Transient moments of joy
When guilt and ambition
And heavy regret didn't
Burden the life of a boy.

*John Bishop*

## *Sutton On Sea*

Our sandshoes used to thunder on the wooden bridge
As we raced each other to the ridge
Stopping to peer in the dyke below
Looking back at the grown-ups - oh so slow!

On up the steps to the promenade
Breathless and laughing the final yard
Doubled with stitch we would spy the sea
And sit on the wall, my cousins and me.

I remember clean beaches and long sunny days
Salty sea air and a shimmering haze
Skimming flat pebbles by the score
Warm breakwater pools for us to explore.

There were sugar pink starfish and long razor shells
Tiny green crabs and seaweedy smells
How energetically our days were filled
With cities and harbours and castles to build.

And on a whim we would run to meet the tide
Exclaiming at the chill as we paddled side by side
Hand in hand wading and splashing
Leaping high as the waves came crashing.

As the smell of hot coffee pervaded the air
Cocooned in towels on a stripy deck chair
We'd hungrily eat our lunch and lie
Stretched in the sun until we were dry.

Then a family game of cricket or catch
A chase down the sands or a rounders match
And arm in arm on the blowy sea shore
Our Nanna and Grandpa were young once more.

*Jennie Dawes*

## The Children's Christmas Concert

The lights like many-coloured eyes
Were focused for this special night.
The stage was set, the curtains drawn,
And clapping hands expressed delight.

The air was almost tangible,
And warm excitement's rosy glow
Tinged chubby cheeks to deeper flush,
Which spread to heaving breasts below.

In breathless pose the children sat,
With shining hair like strands of silk
Of varied shades and varied hues,
Some dark, some red, some buttermilk.

Mary and Joseph in Eastern dress
Moved with practised dignity,
And unaware that they portrayed
The world's most wondrous mystery.

The shepherds in their rainbow robes
Carried their crooks with studied ease.
They pointed to the sequinned stars,
Then made obeisance on their knees.

With a shower of tinsel and a shimmer of gauze,
The angels floated into view.
They spread their wings like butterflies
When shaking loose the drops of dew.

The night was one of wonderment
When magic touched each little face,
And deep enchantment left its mark,
Enshrined forever in its place.

*Celia G Thomas*

## Kids Are Like That . . .

She's a whirlwind.
She's a tomboy.
She's never frilly,
cute or coy . . .
It only takes
two minutes flat,
to wake the baby,
taunt the cat,
make grandmother
drop a stitch,
churn carpet
into football pitch,
wedge her head
in the serving hatch,
turn well-groomed hair
to tousled thatch . . .
She seems devoid
of interaction,
but, as I reach
complete distraction,
and 'juggle' with
the baking tray -
she says, in a
coquettish way,
sweet words which
make my heart succumb . . .
'You'll never know
how much I love you, Mum!'

*Pauline Pullan*

## Christmas Memories

Meeting Santa for the very first time,
Joy at the grotto and pantomime.
A nativity scene, in robes finely clad,
Surprise presents, for Mum and for Dad.
Music and carols on innocent lips,
Snowballs and snowmen, white and crisp.
A wondrous tree, and shining eyes,
Mysterious parcels and delighted cries.
Homemade Christmas cake, best ever seen,
Christmas pudding with custard, jelly and cream.
These magical moments in memory stay
As childhood steals, in silence, away.

*Valerie A Cottier*

## Recollections Of Childhood: A True Story

I've a memory of childhood that was happy and yet sad
Recalling how we lost a wonderland we had
Shall I tell you all about this place of joy and tears -
It was when we found a plot of ground that hadn't been touched for
                                                                                       years.

It became a children's Paradise, our very own playground
It had trees to climb, and blackberries when autumn came around
There were slopes to ride our bikes down and a pond was our boats'
                                                                                         sea
And wavy grass to hide in, and wild flowers growing free.

With none to supervise us or to give us sets of rules -
Such happy hours we spent there, when we came out of school!
What did we need with swings and things the Council Park supplied?
For everyone had much more fun when nature alone provided.

But a day came with Authority cast its beady eye
On our enchanted valley, and so it had to die
They felled the trees, filled in the pond - a Paradise betrayed
And tramping feet crushed grass and flowers in the heaven nature
                                                                                        made

Then it was gone, our Eden - bricks and mortar were displayed
And rows of tidy houses now stand where once we played
I think we felt like Adam and Eve when they were dispossessed
Cast out, exiled and banished from the Garden of the Blest.

*Elsie Karbacz*

## *My Dog*

I grew up with a yellow labrador
Called Min - she was beautiful
A friend and companion wherever we went
She was special, precious and unique

On holiday on the beach, at home on the street
Min would be there by our sides
I've often thought she wasn't a dog
But really an angel in disguise

Whatever our problems, we always told Min
She understood every word of course!
And if you were ill, she'd be laid close by
Comforting by just being there.

Min had a weakness, she loved ice cream
She'd join in the queue at the van
Keeping her place till she got to the front
Then my dad would buy her a cornet

I look at the photos that we took of Min
And I still miss her now, after years
Though I've had other pets that I love very much
I love, and miss Min most of all.

*H Z Billam*

## *Childhood Days*

Didn't have much as a child
Hand me downs, unstyled.
No telly, or radio, but a good mother
No toys, just played with each other.
Mother joined in, kept us happy
Youngsters running, without a nappy
Nothing ever taken for granted
Even slept four in a bed
Grown up better for it now
Not one, has gone off the rail
Nothing we wouldn't do for each.
Will never ever grow out of reach
Now much wiser, and much stronger
A bond between us as we grow fonder.

*Ivy Skinner*

## *Evacuated To Eire, 1940*

Dear Mum, I've arrived
I don't feel too bad
but leaving you all
made me terribly sad.

I felt like a parcel
with a label to show
where I was flying
to whom I should go.

The flight was quite scary
all windows blacked out
we bumped as we landed
and were jostled about.

All is so peaceful
with lights ablaze here
no shelters to run to
no bombs, no all-clear.

There's no rationing of food
we've butter to spread
and a lovely warm smell
of newly-baked bread.

But I want my old room
and I miss all my friends
promise you'll fetch me
when this horrid war ends.

    *Felicity Gill*

## Childhood

'You're horrid,' squealed the little girl.
Her playmates turned away.
She sat alone, her feelings hurt -
They would not let her play!

Why can't we learn that childhood
Is the 'starting block' of life,
Instil in our children - happiness
Not means of causing strife!

Instead of planning wars,
Or living lives beset by greed.
Teach future generations
To consider - those in need!

*Jean McVicar*

## Child Think

Do bears think?

how do birds fly?

what is my 'soul'?

how can you talk to rush?

does one hand clapping have a sound?

please don't tell me to be quiet,

I would know these mysteries of my world.

*Jackie Draysey*

## *The Dawn Of Understanding*

When my Mum was alive,
I used to go to Sunday School.
Reading my bible each evening
Before I fell asleep.

When my Mum died
And left me all alone,
I did not understand
What I had done that was so wrong.

How could He take her away
When, at eleven, I needed her so.
Why? I asked so often then
While I was growing up.

As time went by I realised
Why God took her from me for
No more pain did she endure, and
Now has peace for eternity.

*Margaret Smith*

## Ways Wherein Once I Strolled
## Part 1

Through the garden gate, and over the weed choked channel
To the wicket gate, and the broad meadows beyond;
To climb the steep embankment there to pause
Whilst the mail train speeds by.
Here the path dips, hiding deep pitfalls neath
Reed and rush to ensnare the unwary.
Through the fence onto the blue sward
Inhaling the brine-laden breeze
Wafting the tractors faint chugging; the driver
Hand on wheel; his gaze fixed upon the open furrow,
Heedless of the swarming gulls' clamorous pestering.
And so along the dyke to an inroad of the tide,
Where careful step and measured leap
Regain the path and the vantage of the hill
Here to rest recumbent on the green grass
Rejoicing in the plovers' giddy tumble
Intoxicated by the very breath
                of the vibrant earth.

## Part 2

Exercise books, and all preps paraphernalia
Stowed, Clementi and Kuhlau
Roundly abused for the regulation
Hour; then out on winged feet
Along the perimeter wall to the works
Entrance, up the driveway to the
Satisfying scrunch of gravel, underfoot; thro'
Velvet lawns, where languished
The office staff on hot summer days;
Passed the chauffeurs house
And the Time Office; then
Down onto the track, where cautionary
Wave forestalls a crossing:

The switch thrown, the points shifted,
The long line of Mary Anns*
Squeal and clank their way,
Laden with basic slag, bound
For the tip that engulfed the wilderness
Of the Marsh.

A plume of steam escapes the mill house vent,
And seconds later a loud
Hiss wafted on the breeze, close
Followed by a thunderous concussion
As the ingot, new raised from the
White heat of the soaking pits,
Negotiates the mill.

The few remaining trucks protest
By, pushed by the straining loco,
Clouds of steam clear; safe now to cross and walk on.


* Colloquial name for tipping trucks.

*M Cooper*

## *All Good Things Come To Those Who Wait*

All good things come to those who wait.
Let us consider the way we were,
Let us go back in time and see ourselves there.
Nothing to worry about, with hopes for the future,
Only the present and that is going to last for ever.

Now the time passes amidst our presences,
Our presence together and nothing but ourselves.
A friend perhaps and a friend indeed.
Don't remind me - we can have no pleasant memories here;
No reminder of the past.
No thanks and pity here.

Only what does the future hold? - I don't know.
Sit back; Relax.
All good things come to those who wait.

*Justin Bayless*

## *Looking Back*

When I was a little girl, the years seemed so much longer.
Summer days went on and on, winter's grip seemed stronger.
On frozen ponds in winter's chill, we'd skate and we would slide.
Mums and Dads joined in as well, on sledges we would ride.
But now the ponds are smaller, winters are not so cold,
Kids today will never know the fun we had of old.
Spring followed on, the beech woods woke, the bluebells drifted
through,
We walked mid avenues of green with armfuls of those flowers so
blue.
Primrose day we'd celebrate, with bunches everywhere.
A special chapel service that all the village shared.
But now you can't pick flowers and the woods are smaller too.
The towns have spread their boundaries, and only rambling clubs
walk through.
In prim white gloves and Sunday hats to chapel we would trot,
Two sermons every Sunday, enjoy them, I did not!
With lots of common land around, wild bracken grew head high.
We made our camps and houses, school holidays flew by.
We had no foreign holidays, no 'package deals' for us.
The war put paid to travelling, not even 'seaside' on a bus.
Christmas came so slowly, we longed for Christmas Day.
Hidden presents all revealed, new games for us to play.
We spent the day at grandma's, the family all were there.
The excitement of the Christmas tree, sparkling magic everywhere.
The turkey was so special, we gazed in disbelief.
Christmas pud with sixpences, and we always got one each.
But turkey's not so special now, a meat for everyday.
Christmas is so commercial and the magic's gone away.
I now look back and forward too, I've enjoyed my life so far.
Space travel next, a lunar trip, or hitch my spaceship to a star?

*Mary Baty*

## *Class Politics*

Quite clearly I remember, a crane on my birthday when I was four.
Going to school the year after,
followed by instant confrontation with headmistress or headmaster.
False accusations of vandalism, of throwing stones in the school
swimming pool
and breaking, ripping the pool lining.
My mind a state of confusion, scared to go into the classroom,
running away, out through the gates each morning.
Made to go back; tears, red face, weeping, lost . . .
Angry voices shouting, I recall everything,
and then better things, improved situation;
good at history, English, maths.
Liked games, but left out of the school team.
Class politics - who's friends with who matters.
No girls; didn't like those,
or liked them but couldn't admit it.
A sign of weakness;
that's what I thought, but I learnt.
Recollections of childhood, of Action Men, little soldiers and Airfix
models.
Gave all that up when I discovered music; The Clash, The Pistols, The
Buzzcocks.
No looking back after that.
That was the start of something else, the next stage - adolescence,
and childhood became a thing of the past, something strange and
distant.
Everything changed, some things for the better, some things for the
worse.
Dreams were shattered, innocence lost,
but something came in its place,
something exciting, magical and vibrant,
something I understood, well almost.

*Andy Botterill*

*Innocence*

Innocence is the key.
it is the only way to connect.
It is timeless.
It will swallow all your faults
and bad ideas.
It will keep you in contact
with the rolling waves, the new born sun.
It will take you through black and white,
it will run out of this pen.
It will give you everything,
if you will not hide from it.
If you will not build up barriers,
to block it out;
it will show its strength,
which will astound you.
It makes all the laughs, which you hear,
laughing at it.

*J Walker*

*Tyranny*

When we were walking home from School,
The big boys used to thump me,
Push me around, tease me, take my cap.
They threw the cap, one to another,
And made me run about, and beg for it.
Then they'd throw it over the hedge,
Into the field, and make me fetch it.
I used to take a long time to go to the gate,
And down the hedge, and sometimes they'd get bored
With me, and run past our house, and go on home.
I knew why they picked on me. -
When Sir asked them things they couldn't answer,
He used to send for me, - to sting their pride.
I wished I could be brave enough to say I didn't know,
But he'd be sure I knew, and seize me by the coat,
And put his face near mine, and snarl and shout,
So his moustache bristled, and bits of spit hung on it.
His breath smelt sour, of old pipe-smoke.
He caught me once - now I'd rather face the boys.
Then, one day, they threw my cap over the opposite hedge
Into Mrs Flint's garden! I cried. I didn't dare to go
And fetch it. 'I'd have to ask my foster-mum
To go and ask for it.' But the boys surprised me.
They gathered by the gate, eeny, meeny, miny, mo-ed,
And he who was 'it', opened the gate, rushed in,
And got my cap! He threw it at me, shouting
'Now you needn't tell her' and they ran off!

They left me alone for about a week.
Afterwards, they still teased me, pushed me around
Sometimes - but they never took my cap again.
Slowly it got less. I sometimes wonder why . . . .

*Robert T Collins*

## *Reflections Of Childhood*

Childhood - so many memories crossed my mind!
Long, lazy days, playing for hours on end,
Freedom to wander unafraid,
Happy times with friends;
The joy of reading, which is with me still.
Times, too, of unhappiness -
The death of a beloved dog,
The loss of things held dear.
Sights, sounds and smells of a different age -
The clip-clop of horses' hooves along the road,
The metallic ring of the miners' clogs
As they hurried by for their early shift;
An airship in the sky,
The hot, damp smell of washday.
Icy patterns in windows on frosty mornings,
Children's Hour on the wireless,
Singing round the piano on winter nights;
Ice-cream from 'Stop-me-and-buy-one!'
Harvest fields with their sweet-scented stooks;
Childhood illnesses with a fire in the bedroom
Creating patterns on the ceiling.
Above all the warmth of a loving family.

*E M Spencer*

## *The Hermit*

What happened to you hermit man
What happened in the sun,
No trace of life within your shack,
It seems your days are done.

A boulder here, an old tin can,
The roof has even gone.
A sad and lonely battered hat
Gives thought to dream upon.

Was there a love within your life,
Why sought you refuge here,
To sit upon your lonely step
Perhaps your thoughts to clear.

Although you weren't aware of it
By chance you were my friend,
And gave me joy within my heart
Until the very end.

I wish you well where e'er you are,
Please think about me too.
You looked my way and smiled at me
With twinkling eyes of blue.

Though evidence has gone with time,
I feel your presence still,
And you'll remain for ever more
My hermit on the hill.

*Phillippa Benson*

## 38 Lewisham Park

More garden than park, yet a world to me
at five and let loose in the Eden green,
I return to its sinuous paths and see
the now clipped shrubs within a lost demesne.

On this lawn was my first bike ride towards
the hollow where the November hangers
scared me and, in sandals and shaking swords
of wood, we played at war with loud clangours.

The house still stands framed by shedding chestnuts -
the way is no longer a puddled gravel.
The tree-hung crescent turns its back and shuts
out the shopping street din through time's travel.

At the park's far edge three tower blocks hide
the site of the school, my first might-have-been.
Nearby, the war memorial where with pride
we stood excited, waving the new Queen.

Uncreased spectres of past visitors stand
by Edwardian gable and clapboard fence,
my uncle who saw this as Alice-land:
mirrored windows reflecting the silence.

And the hunter stalking the leafy park
and my bedroom in search of prey awake
still, and the young song of the morning lark
as I open my eyes and meet heart-ache.

*F Pettitt*